Veronica K. Needler
5610 Crawfordsville Road
Building 17
Indianapolis, IN 46224

PRINCIPLES OF

PSYCHOANALYTIC

PSYCHOTHERAPY

PRINCIPLES OF PSYCHOANALYTIC PSYCHOTHERAPY

A Manual for Supportive-Expressive Treatment

LESTER LUBORSKY

Basic Books, Inc., Publishers

NEW YORK

Library of Congress Cataloging in Publication Data

Luborsky, Lester, 1920–
  Principles of psychoanalytic psychotherapy.

  References: p. 241
  Includes index.
  1. Psychoanalysis. 2. Psychotherapy. I. Title.
[DNLM: 1. Psychoanalytic therapy. WM 460.6 L929p]
RC504.L83 1984   616.89'17   83-45377
ISBN 0-465-06328-4

To Three Generations

To the First: Sigmund Freud,

the founder of most of these methods.

To the Second: The Menninger Foundation's mentors,

the transmitters of skill in using them.

To the Third: Psychotherapy researchers,

the persevering evaluators of these methods.

Contents

Contents

Contents

PART II
The Manual

Contents

PART III

Appendices

Contents

Foreword

Psychotherapy, generally speaking, has been shown to be effective. Most people who seek help for heterogeneous arrays of symptoms—crippling compulsions, paralyzing obsessions, depression, anxieties, and bodily aberrations without organic cause—are indeed helped by the psychotherapeutic encounter. The goals of these treatments have now extended beyond their original aim (which was the cure of recognized nosological entities, perhaps even diseases, such as obsessive–compulsive neurosis or hysteria), to personality or character problems, and even beyond those to "optimizing" social and interpersonal effectiveness. Regardless of the patient's condition, whether disease or plight, psychotherapy has shown itself to be helpful, as several comprehensive reviews have documented (e.g., Luborsky, Singer, and Luborsky 1975; Bergin and Lambert 1978; Smith, Glass, and Miller 1980).

In spite of the demonstrated general superiority of psychotherapy over no treatment, formidable problems for evaluation remain. They include the heterogeneity of conditions for which people seek relief, the array of psychotherapeutic methods claiming effectiveness, and the multitude of therapists with their own theoretical persuasions. All of these factors demand more precise and specific answers to the question of what therapy, administered by what therapist, is effective for which patients with what conditions. The technology of psychotherapy, unlike, for example, that of physical medicine, is "soft." It depends on words. Yet the orchestration of the techniques requires deftness, subtlety, and integrity in the same measure as that needed by the skilled musician. As Hamlet forthrightly reminded the meddling Rosencrantz and Guildenstern, "you would pluck out the heart of my mystery, you would sound me from my lowest note to the top of my compass; and there is much music, excellent voice in this little organ, yet you cannot make it speak. 'Sblood, do you think I am easier to be played on than a pipe?"

Because of the wide array of psychotherapies and of the large number of people seeking help from psychotherapy, there is an accelerating movement toward demonstrating the efficacy and safety of these methods. Among the difficulties this movement confronts is the phalanx of over 250 name brands of psychotherapy (Herink 1980) and over 150 categories of disorders for which psychotherapy is sought or recommended; a matrix with 37,500 cells! Yet from a consumer's view, it seems only reasonable to begin to determine which therapies administered by which therapists work for which conditions.

Psychotherapy has been called a craft. This can only describe the way in which the procedure is administered, applied, or conducted. To determine whether or not a craftsman is skilled requires a clear statement of the operations of the special craft. Psychodynamic psychotherapy, stemming from psychoanalysis, is one of the most frequently employed of psychotherapies and, curiously, one of the least systematically studied for its efficacy.

This book provides a necessary tool for studies on the effectiveness of psychodynamically oriented psychotherapy. In this manual, Lester Luborsky, an experienced therapist, psychoanalyst, and distinguished teacher and researcher, sets down the basic operations of "supportive–expressive psychoanalytically oriented psychotherapy." He discusses the treatment of disorders in which people work against their own self-interest in ways that elude their own otherwise intelligent awareness. An exploration of motives, of the continuity of purposes in a person's life, methods of confronting oneself and others, and of the nature of the relationship between patient and therapist (the "transference"), form the basic operations of the therapy. Dr. Luborsky's clear exposition of the criteria for establishing whether and how supportive–expressive psychoanalytically oriented psychotherapy is being practiced in a particular instance makes it possible to judge the extent to which a therapist has applied these techniques and the adequacy with which he or she has applied them. With the aid of this manual, a researcher can go on to study the extent to which any of the elements of the treatment or any combination of them are necessary for a "good" therapeutic outcome in specific disorders.

The manual has yet another important function. It can be used both in the training of therapists and by experienced therapists wishing to sharpen their skills. This is because it adds a significant orienting schema to the necessary ingredients and processes that are required in this kind of therapy. This orienting schema demystifies the operations, and thereby makes possible for the learner a greater mastery of the therapeutic technique.

In addition to the clearly stated outline of the therapeutic process and the edifying examples that illustrate the steps, Dr. Luborsky explores the theory of the therapy lucidly, articulately, and comprehensibly. His division of the therapy into specific and nonspecific factors is a helpful one. It makes possible a further exploration of the special ameliorative factors in the treatment. His careful focus on the nature of the therapeutic relationship and the responses of both patient and therapist to it, extend an understanding of the nature and use of transference phenomena through his elaboration of the core conflictual relationship theme. Psychotherapy researchers will find in this manual many gems modestly stated, such as statements on how to observe therapeutic movement and operational criteria of unconscious psychological processes.

This is a welcome book. It fills a need for psychotherapy outcome research while providing a didactic tool and a set of theoretical hypotheses about the psychodynamics of one kind of change, namely, that intentionally embarked upon in the context of a relationship between two people.

PHILIP S. HOLZMAN, PH.D.
Professor of Psychology
Harvard University
Cambridge, Massachusetts

Preface

For many years this introduction to the principles of psychoanalytically oriented psychotherapy was primarily used in the training of psychotherapists at the University of Pennsylvania's Department of Psychiatry. Then, less than a decade ago a small revolution in psychotherapy research style demanded that an official "manual" be devised for each psychotherapy so that methods and theories could effectively be implemented and compared. The manual from which this book is derived was one of the first such manuals. The theories, techniques, and clinical strategies presented here are based on years of clinical research. The result is a carefully tested guide to the practice of psychoanalytically oriented psychotherapy for practitioners, researchers, and supervisors.

My aim has been to assemble in a manual format the most representative and commonly used techniques in the practice of psychoanalytically oriented psychotherapy. Since there are so many accounts of this kind of psychotherapy, it is important to describe for the reader how this particular version came about and what is special about both the therapy and its manual in comparison with other therapies and their manuals.

The foundations of the manual rest heavily on my learning experiences with classical psychoanalysis and psychoanalytically oriented psychotherapy during 13 years at the Menninger Foundation (1947–59). There, classical psychoanalysis and the Menninger Foundation's supportive-expressive psychoanalytically oriented psychotherapy were the two most practiced psychotherapies. The term *supportive-expressive* comes from that locale. As used in this manual it is not a new version of psychoanalytically oriented psychotherapy, but rather it contains its essential features. The term *supportive-expressive* refers to the two main classes of techniques in the treatment: the supportive ones derive from the supportive relationship with the therapist; the expressive ones derive from the means of understanding what the patient expresses.

My earliest experiences with this psychotherapy were the most formative, and took place during five successive years with five different colleagues as supervisors each of whom were psychiatrists who practiced both psychotherapy and psychoanalysis: Drs. Lewis Robbins, Michalina Fabian, Irving Kartus, Albert Owers, and Carl Epstein. Naturally, therefore, I am highly appreciative of the system of yearly rotation of supervision by colleagues at the Menninger Foundation, as well as the opportunity over the five-year period to experience what psychoanalysis was like from the patient's viewpoint. The input from three supervisors of my psychoanalytic training at the Topeka Psychoanalytic Institute is also obviously reflected in this manual: Drs. Otto Fleishmann, Petrinella Tibout, and Ishak Ramzy. Dr. Fleishmann, for example, impressed me with his precept to have patience and to listen to the patient and wait until one had "the material" before drawing conclusions and deciding what to interpret.

Some of my colleagues in those years who influenced my theories of therapy and psychotherapeutic technique were: Drs. Rudolph Ekstein, Karl Menninger, William Pious, Helmut Kaiser, Jan Frank, Philip Holzman, Merton Gill, David Rapaport, George Klein, Herbert Schlesinger, Robert R. Holt, Robert Wallerstein, Walter Kass, Margaret Brenman, Benjamin Rubenstein, Paul Bergman, Roy Schafer, Martin Mayman, Otto Kernberg, Gardner Murphy, Lois Murphy, and

Howard Shevrin. I believe my therapeutic style became a personal admixture of what they offered.

Aspects of my style also came from my supervision of psychiatric residents and psychologists in the Department of Psychiatry at the University of Pennsylvania during my years in Philadelphia after 1959. One of the psychiatrists I supervised, Dr. Perry Berman, had a part in instigating the train of ideas which eventually led me to the core conflictual relationship theme method (CCRT), which will be described in chapter 7 and appendix 4. I remember the times he insisted that there was more to the process of understanding the main relationship theme than I had been telling him. It was not enough for me to say that one listens and the understanding comes, but that I should spell out the principles guiding the understanding. I tried to do that and eventually came up with the principles of the CCRT.

Some of the examples of the technical principles in the manual derived from these experiences in providing supervision. In addition, it was the supervisees' appreciation of the early versions of the manual, then called *The Task of the Psychotherapist* (1973), which encouraged me to copyright it on April 5, 1976. I was heartened as well by the way in which they reciprocated my appreciation of them by suggesting me as the recipient of the 1977 Earl Bond Award for Excellence in teaching in the Department of Psychiatry.

The final precipitant to the decision to publish the manual came in the summer of 1979 after two old friends and Menninger Foundation colleagues read a draft of the manual. Dr. Philip Holzman was enthusiastic about having it published together with a historical introduction and more examples to ensure the learning of the principles, as in a programmed learning text. Dr. Gerald Aronson expertly applied pressure to the theoretical scaffolding of the supportive–expressive (SE) principles and then led me socratically toward ways of strengthening them.

The most accessible layer of the foundations for the chosen treatment techniques came from psychotherapy research, both my own and that of others. However, these influences on practice were less than one might have expected considering my decades of involvement in psychotherapy research. In 1969, I even wrote a skeptical article on this theme: "Research Cannot Yet Influence Clinical Practice." My view parallels Carl Rogers' observation that his own psychotherapy research (which was prodigous in productivity and diversity) had had little influence on his clinical practice (personal communication, about 1960).

In the last decade, however, psychotherapy research has begun to have a greater impact on clinical practice. I am about ready to disavow my 1969 view because several lines of research have much influenced parts of this manual. Three main examples of such research sources are evident in it: (1) the predictive value of the helping alliance (Luborsky 1976a; Morgan, Luborsky, Crits-Christoph, Curtis, and Solomon 1981; Luborsky Crits-Christoph, Alexander, Margolis, and Cohen 1983); (2) the guidance to understanding of the transference patterns provided by the core conflictual relationship theme method (CCRT) (Luborsky 1977); and (3) the implications for matching patients and therapists by different methods of assignment (Luborsky and McLellan 1981; McLellan, Luborsky, Woody, O'Brien, and Druley 1983; and McLellan, Luborsky, O'Brien, Druley and Woody, 1983). For partial support of these research studies I wish to acknowledge United States Public Health Service Research Scientist Award 40710.

Colleagues, friends, relatives, and combinations of these have had a helping relationship in this manual's maturation and arrival at publication. Outstanding among them were

Preface

Philip Holzman, Leslie Alexander, Marjorie Cohen, Arthur Auerbach, Gerald Aronson, George Woody, Frederic J. Levine, Stanley Greenspan, Ellen Berman, Marshall Edelson, John Docherty, Paul Gerin, Ellen Luborsky, Ruth Samson Luborsky, Lise Luborsky, and Peter Luborsky. I want to thank Philip Holzman particularly for writing the foreword, and for his capacity to unite the functions of a fine foreword with those of friendship. Jo Ann Miller and Theresa Craig of Basic Books gave the manuscript a final masterly organizational assist.

Two recent prepublication trials of the manual helped increase its utility: (1) the psychiatric residents in their fourth postgraduate year and postdoctoral psychology fellows at the University of Pennsylvania, Department of Psychiatry (1982–83), Dr. Edward Schweizer, Chief Resident; (2) the seminar at Universität Ulm, Department of Psychotherapy (December 1981 and December 1982, organized by Dr. Horst Kächele and Dr. Helmut Thomä).

Because of the mutual learning that goes on between supervisor and therapist, I wish to especially acknowledge the therapists, both faculty and fellows, with whom I spent a year or more discussing their patients (not a complete list):

Linda Altman-Fischer, M.D.
Thomas Aronson, M.D.
Minna Baker, Ph.D.
Henry C. Berger, M.D.
Ellen Berman, M.D.
Perry Berman, M.D.
Stephen Billick, M.D.
Charles Billings, M.D.
William Binstock, M.D.
Oliver Bjorksten, M.D.
Jack Brandes, M.D.
Susan Bryant, M.D.
Victor Burt, M.D.
Cheryl Cantrell, M.D.
Anna Rose Childress, Ph.D.
Cathryn Clary, M.D.
Robert Cohn, M.D.
James Congdon, M.D.
Leo Dorozynsky, M.D.
Philip Feldman, M.D.
Gladys Fenichel, M.D.
Catherine Fine, Ph.D.
Joseph Fishbein, M.D.
Pamela Frazier, M.D.
Daniel Frohwirth, M.D.
Thomas Gable, M.D.
Gary Glass, M.D.

Joel Glass, M.D.
Mark Giesecke, M.D.
Igor Grant, M.D.
Rubin Gur, Ph.D.
Charles Hanson, M.D. J.D.
David Hartman, M.D.
Joan Harvey, Ph.D.
D. Daniel Hunt, M.D.
Aaron Katcher, M.D.
Kenneth Kessler, M.D.
Mitchel Kling, M.D.
Richard Kluft, M.D.
Gary Lande, M.D.
Elizabeth Liao, M.D.
Marc Lipschutz, M.D.
George Luedke, M.D.
Martha McClintock, Ph.D.
Philip J. Mechanick, M.D.
Richard Merkel, M.D.
Gary Mihalik, M.D.
Laurence Miller, M.D.
Carol Newlin, M.D., Ph.D.
Herbert Nickens, M.D.
James Nocks, M.D.
Samuel Okpaku, M.D., Ph.D.
Sydnor Penick, M.D.
Wilfred Postel, M.D.

David Pruitt, M.D.
Edwin Rascoe, M.D.
Stephen I. Ring, M.D.
Alan Ringold. M.D.
Alberto Rish, M.D.
Baird Ritter, M.D.
Meyer Rothbart, M.D.
Thomas Scaramella, M.D.
Dean Schuyler, M.D.
Edward Schweizer, M.D.
Anita Settle Hole, Ph.D.
Stephen Stern, M.D.
James Stinnet, M.D.
Albert J. Stunkard, M.D.
David Sydney, M.D.
Levon D. Tashjian, M.D.
Robert Toborowsky, M.D.
John A. Turner, M.D.
John Valentine, M.D.
Paul van Ravenswaay, M.D.
Tony Villeco, Ph.D.
Frederick L. Whipple, M.D.
William Wieland, M.D.
Andrew Winokur, M.D.
Carol Wolman, M.D.

Lester Luborsky, Ph.D.
Philadelphia, PA
January, 1984

PART I

The Background
and Use of
the Manual

1

The Purposes of the Book
and the Qualities of
the Treatment

The Purposes of the Book

Psychoanalytically oriented psychotherapy is a widely used term for a widely used form of psychotherapy. In the United States, it is the most usual form of psychotherapy practiced both in outpatient psychiatric clinics and in private practice (Feldman, Lorr, and Russell 1958; Henry, Sims, and Spray 1973). Even with the increased use of behavior therapies (Brady 1970) and existential psychotherapies (Karasu 1981), the practice of psychoanalytically oriented psychotherapy has not declined; instead, newer treatments have been added to the large variety already available (Parloff 1979).

Despite the widespread practice of psychoanalytically oriented psychotherapy, it suffers, as all other psychotherapies do, from a deficiency in tested knowledge as to why it is usually helpful and why it occasionally does not work. Research on the relative benefits of different types of psychotherapy needs more discerning and more powerful methods than those in the many past studies (reviewed in Luborsky, Singer and Luborsky 1975, and Smith, Glass, and Miller 1980). The methods should include at the minimum, (1) a definitive description of the techniques of each form of psychotherapy; (2) a detailed guide to the therapist on the practice of the techniques; and (3) a measure of the degree to which the therapist conforms to the techniques in his or her practice. The last requirement has been almost routinely neglected.

This book tries to relieve some of the pressing problems of the field, by fulfilling these three minimal research requirements as well as the five additional contributions which follow:

1. A DEFINITIVE ACCOUNT OF PSYCHOANALYTICALLY ORIENTED PSYCHOTHERAPY

The manual gives the core principles of this form of therapy which is based on Freud's recommendations for psychoanalytic technique ([1911, 1912a and b, 1913a, 1914, 1915]1958 v.12), together with the recommendations by later authoritative sources based on many decades of use and development, especially at the Menninger Foundation. The distinctive essence of this type of therapy, is discussed in the second half of this chapter and in chapter 2.

2. A TREATMENT GUIDE IN A MANUAL FORMAT

The presentation satisfies the three essential requirements of the psychotherapy treatment manual format: (a) the treatment recommendations should be as complete as the type of treatment permits, and it should state the main techniques which are integral to the treatment. (b) The manual should make clear the treatment principles and the operations which the therapist is supposed to perform. This is best accomplished by presenting each technique as concretely as possible as well as by providing examples of each technique. (c) The manual should have an accompanying set of scales to measure the degree to which the therapists have complied with its main techniques (see appendix 5).

Although recommendations for doing psychotherapy are plentiful, this manual is the very first for psychoanalytically oriented psychotherapy which meets these format requirements (Luborsky and DeRubeis in press). With the exception of those for the classical behavior therapies, it is one of the first full-scale manuals of any form of psychotherapy.

3. A SET OF SCALES FOR MEASURING THERAPISTS' CONFORMITY TO THE MANUAL'S RECOMMENDATIONS

The degree to which the therapist has mastered the manual and is, therefore, able to follow its recommendations can be evaluated by independent judges applying the manual-based rating forms to samples of the therapist's sessions (see appendix 5). These forms are based in part on Luborsky, Woody, McLellan, O'Brien, and Rosenzweig (1982).

4. A TRAINING TOOL FOR THERAPISTS, SUPERVISORS, AND TEACHERS

The manual format is a useful aid in the training of therapists, it helps experienced therapists improve their skills, and it is a resourceful companion to have along during supervision. The scales for measuring the treatment techniques can be used to judge when a therapist is able to perform the therapy in conformity with the manual and has fulfilled the goal of the training.

Furthermore, the manual is written with special empathy for the therapist's task. It demonstrates this empathy through its delineation of principles the therapist should follow in understanding the patient's communications. Throughout the history of SE therapy, the process by which the therapist draws inferences from the patient's communications has been largely neglected (Ramzy 1974; Ramzy and Shevrin 1976).

The aim of the manual—to delineate the principles the therapist follows in understanding the patient's motives—is especially appropriate. It fits the mark of a psychoanalytic orientation that the therapist tries to achieve "understanding of intentionality from the patient's point of view" (Klein 1970). The manual presents a scheme for achieving this understanding through a refinement of the clinical method called the core conflictual relationship theme (CCRT) method (see chapter 7). This method provides principles for understanding the theme of the patient's wishes, needs, and intentions in regard to the main people, including the therapist, with whom he or she interacts during the psychotherapy. The understanding of the theme can then serve as a guide for the therapist's interpretative responses to the patient.

5. A GUIDE TO EVALUATING AND STRENGTHENING THE SUPPORTIVE RELATIONSHIP

Chapter 6 presents such a guide. It is based partly on clinical–quantitative research which has shown the benefits to the patient of a helping alliance. This alliance is defined as the degree to which the patient experiences the relationship with the therapist as helpful in achieving his or her goals.

6. A MANUAL FOR BOTH SHORT-TERM AND OPEN-ENDED PSYCHOTHERAPY

Special directions for time-limited therapy are designated by the notation SE-TL. When no notation is given in the text, the directions refer to both forms. The inclusion of SE-TL instructions increases the present work's value for research studies, since investigators are attracted by the convenience of brief, time-limited treatments. It is also an advantage in terms of broader applicability to patients in clinics where short-term treatment is not only suitable but often advantageous.

7. A TREATMENT ADAPTABLE TO A BROAD RANGE OF PATIENTS

The usual adaptation is a patient-specific mix of supportiveness and expressiveness. At the Menninger Foundation, for example, it is even used for patients who are hospitalized and treated by both a hospital doctor and a psychotherapist. For these patients, the therapist is relieved by the hospital doctor of some aspects of patient care such as the administering of medication (guides for SE plus medication appear in chapter 10).

8. AN INTEGRATION OF CLINICAL AND RESEARCH FINDINGS

As much of quantitative psychotherapy research findings is integrated throughout the text as is relevant at the present stage of such research. There is more research backing for the efficacy of the treatment in this manual and its principles than is generally realized.

The Essence of Psychoanalytically Oriented Psychotherapy

Characteristics of psychoanalytically oriented psychotherapy can be recognized through comparisons with its nearest relatives. The most distinctive features of psychoanalytically oriented psychotherapy can be seen by looking at it along side of its parent discipline, psychoanalysis. In fact, most of the accounts of psychoanalytically oriented psychotherapy in the last few decades define it through its contrasts with psychoanalysis. Since Freud ([1911, 1912a and b, 1913a, 1914, and 1915]1958) first spelled out his treatment recommendations for psychoanalysis in the six famous techniques papers, these have formed the ur source for the formal definition of classical psychoanalysis. That mode of psychotherapy has had several excellent explications and reformulations while still remaining recognizable as classical psychoanalysis; for example, Fenichel (1941), Stone (1951), and Menninger and Holzman (1973).

In the period since Freud's innovation of psychoanalysis, two primary motives have impelled the differentiation of psychoanalytically oriented psychotherapies from classical psychoanalysis (although the offspring have retained obvious resemblances to the parent). The first, and earliest, of these differentiations, made by Ferenczi (1920) and Rank (1936), were fashioned to satisfy the needs of both patients and therapists to shorten the length of psychoanalysis. Alexander and French (1946) continued the drive toward shortening psychoanalytic treatments with the aim of making them more affordable than classical psychoanalysis. They were often shortened to within the usual range of brief psychotherapy. According to Butcher and Koss (1978), "Today . . . 25 sessions is the upper limit of 'brief' therapy, with as many clinicians recommending . . . one to six sessions as the longer 10 to 25 sessions." Another class of psychoanalytically oriented psychotherapies was worked out in the early 1940s during the Second World War by Grinker and Spiegel (1944, 1945) and Lindemann (1944) as a basis for crisis interventions. These procedures gave further impetus to the very short-term methods, for they could be applied in one to three sessions in situations where immediate intervention was required and little time was available.

The second motive for differentiating from classical psychoanalysis related to the need for a more versatile psychotherapy in terms of types of patients. Psychoanalytically oriented psy-

8

chotherapy is readily adaptable to a broad range of patients, including those with poor psychological health who may have difficulty in tolerating the classical psychoanalytic treatment structure.

THE DISTINCTIVE TREATMENT PRINCIPLES

Since there is no one complete source, this selection of treatment principles is derived from a small sample of the scores of published accounts of the nature of this form of psychotherapy. Since the most practiced of the techniques associated with psychoanalytically oriented psychotherapy are included, the sample is weighted toward the more clinical rather than the more theoretical accounts. The statement of the principles as well as the entire manual is also fairly free of unessential metapsychological language.

The principles were extracted from this sample of accounts: Bergmann and Hartman (1977); Bibring (1954); Freud ([1911, 1912a and b, 1913a, 1914, and 1915]1958); Gill (1951, 1954); Greenson (1967); Hollender (1965); Luborsky, Fabian, Hall, Ticho, and Ticho (1958); Schlesinger (1969); Stone (1961); Wallerstein, Robbins, Sargent, and Luborsky (1956); Wallerstein (in press).

Supportive–expressive psychoanalytically oriented psychotherapy has a long history. It has been one of the standard treatments used at the Menninger Foundation, in essentially the form described in this manual, since about 1940 (Wallerstein et al. 1956). It has been called supportive–expressive (or expressive–supportive) psychoanalytically oriented psychotherapy, depending on which techniques predominate. The version presented here will be referred to as SE hereafter, an abbreviation which concretely sums up its combination of supportive and expressive techniques. These are the main, distinctive characteristics of SE, and an asterisk (*) before a characteristic marks it as especially important.

*1. Clinical Psychoanalytic Principles.

The well-known clinical principles of psychoanalysis are used; foremost among these is guidance by the manifestations of transference (chapter 2).

*2. Expressive Techniques.

They are standard psychoanalytic interpretive techniques. They set the stage for the patient to express his or her thoughts and feelings and for the therapist and patient then to listen and reflect on them. The understanding obtained is the vehicle for changing what needs to be changed. The thoughts and feelings expressed gradually make explicit what the patient is doing which is self-hurtful and may, therefore, need to be changed. The assumption is that the patient is behaving in ways which could be controlled if the person knew more about what he or she was doing (i.e., this assumption involves the idea of unconscious factors determining behavior). The most telling revelations about what the patient is doing come from the reexperiencing of the central early relationship problems in the relationship with the therapist, that is, in the transference.

In classical psychoanalysis, expressive techniques are supposed to be used continually, particularly for the analysis of the successive editions of the transference which are activated in the treatment. For many patients in SE, this use of expressive techniques is the same as it would be in classical analysis. But for some patients in SE, expressive techniques may be relatively less used and supportive techniques more used, since some patients in SE are more limited in their ability to profit from expressive techniques.

3. Supportive Aspects.

The term refers to the aspects of SE psychotherapy which are reflected in the patient's experience of both the treatment and the relationship with the therapist as helpful. These supportive aspects tend to be noncognitive in the sense that they are not primarily aimed at providing understanding. Most derive from the treatment structure, for example, the regular appointments, the concern with identifying the patient's treatment goals, and the fact that the therapist and the patient are working toward fulfillment of those goals. Some common, positive transference expectations also tend to further the supportive aspects of the treatment. These supportive aspects which are present in SE, as they are in other psychotherapies, and are even present in classical psychoanalysis (which can be, and often is, experienced by the patient as very supportive), may be referred to as part of the nonspecific curative factors.

In addition to the naturally supportive aspects, SE makes explicit provision for facilitating the supportive conditions for some patients at some times (chapter 6). Such flexibly planned facilitation is widely accepted by those who subscribe to the SE philosophy, but its use is not without risk. The primary risk is that such facilitation will take the place of adherence to appropriate expressive techniques and thus limit the patient's development.

4. Nonreliance on Advice Giving.

Refraining from giving advice has a recognized place in psychoanalytically oriented psychotherapy (Bibring 1954). In practice, there is evidence of relatively little advice giving in SE as compared to other psychotherapies (see chapter 3).

5. Face-to-Face Position of Therapist and Patient.
This is always true of psychoanalytically oriented psychotherapy. Only classical psychoanalysis uses the couch, with the analyst sitting behind the patient as an aid to free association and to avoid the distraction to the patient of having the analyst in view.

6. Length of Treatment and Time Structure.
SE can be either time open-ended (TO) or time limited (TL). The term *time open-ended* is used rather than *time unlimited,* since it is more descriptive of the time aspects of SE. The term *time open-ended* correctly implies that the end will be decided as the participants go along in the treatment, while the term *unlimited* implies that there is no consideration of time and that there is no limit. TL tends to be from 6 to 25 sessions; TO tends to be from a few months to several years.

7. Number of Sessions Per Week.
The usual frequency is once or twice per week. Classical psychoanalysis is almost always four or five sessions per week.

The Plan of the Book

The book is in two parts and includes an appendix. Part I sets out the reasons for manuals; the nature of the therapy and how it relates to the theory; the preparation of the patient; and selection of patients and therapists.

Part II gives an account of supportive–expressive psychoanalytically oriented psychotherapy (SE) via an exposition of its principles, with examples, in a manual format.

The appendices provide special tools to help facilitate the practice of the therapy, including a sample interview for preparing the patient, a sample scoring of the core conflictual relationship theme (CCRT), and a set of rating scales to measure the degree to which the therapist engaged in the behaviors that befit a supportive–expressive psychoanalytically oriented psychotherapist. The chapters on the steps in SE psychotherapy follow the approximate time-ordered sequence of the SE psychotherapy treatment system:

1. The patient is prepared before treatment for the opportunity for psychotherapy (chapter 4).
2. The early treatment sessions are the time to set the goals and to explain the treatment arrangements; a relationship of trust and rapport begins to be established; and the process of formulating the main relationship problem gets under way (chapter 5).
3. The relationship's state of supportiveness is attended to and fostered when necessary (chapter 6).
4. The expressive component, which is aimed at achieving an understanding of the symptoms and accompanying relationship problems, is pursued as is appropriate (chapter 7, 8).
5. The conclusion of the treatment is dealt with by methods that are calculated to maintain the gains of the treatment (chapter 9).

It is difficult to anticipate all the steps of SE treatment. As Freud ([1913a]1958) concluded in terms of his well-known analogy between chess and psychotherapy, we know only some of the opening and closing moves, and for the rest we have only intuitively applied guidelines. Therefore, "this gap in instruction can only be filled by diligent study of games fought out by masters" (p. 123). In the course of the manual, not only will the opening and closing steps be detailed, but some of the intervening ones as well. These five steps and the steps within each are intended to give as much order to the process as possible. It should be remembered throughout, however, that it is not the primary aim just to follow the order of the steps. A similar issue in religious observance was resolved thus: The Talmud states (p. 49, *Sanhedrin*, beginning of the sixth chapter) that when various lists appear, many of them do not really imply a necessary sequence; not even for the Day of Atonement service is there a necessary sequence. It is only important that there be a "change of heart." So, too, although the SE techniques have a logical sequence, it is not an inflexible one. Rather, it is more important that the therapist and the patient keep in mind the idea of helping the patient get where he or she is going in terms of the changes that anticipate and accompany the attaining of the patient's goals.

2

The Psychoanalytic
Theory of
Psychotherapeutic Change

The SE psychotherapy that has just been described, derives from the psychoanalytic theory of psychotherapeutic change. Since this chapter focuses on those aspects of the theory with the greatest consensus among the authoritative sources, the chapter title seemed justified: *"The* Psychoanalytic Theory . . ." rather than *"A* Psychoanalytic Theory. . . ." Certain sources were especially beneficial in tracing its derivation, and the readers may also wish to consult them: Bibring (1954); Fenichel (1941); Freud ([1911, 1912a and b, 1913a, 1914, and 1915] 1958); Luborsky and Schimek (1964); Menninger and Holzman (1973); and Stone (1951).

Like any theory of change through psychotherapy, the psychoanalytic theory of change has to answer two broad questions:

1. What is the entity that changes?
2. How does the change come about?

The answers constitute the psychoanalytic theory of change and are summed up in table 2.1.

TABLE 2.1

Changes in SE Psychoanalytically Oriented Psychotherapy, and How Such Changes Come About

	How the Changes Come About	
What Changes	Patient	Therapist and Treatment Conditions
1. P's increased understanding of the symptoms and the related core conflictual relationship theme (CCRT) problems, some of which the P had been unaware of. The understanding leads to changes in the symptoms and greater mastery over the deleterious expressions of the CCRT problems as well as some changes in the components of the CCRT.	Through P's ability to become involved in achieving understanding of the core conflictual relationship problems, to persist in their working through in the relationship with T, and perhaps to understand the relevant past relationships.	Through T's ability to involve P in self-expression and in achieving understanding of the CCRT problems and to persist in their working through in the relationship with T. Some understanding is also usually sought by T for those past relationships which are relevant to current ones.
2. P's increased sense of having an ally in the struggle to overcome aspects of the repetitive, self-defeating CCRT problems.	Through P's ability to form a helping alliance with the T.	Through T's ability to facilitate P's experience of an helping alliance by providing support.
3. P's more internalized control-mastery system in relation to the CCRT so that the gains are persistent after the treatment.	Through P's ability to internalize the gains of the treatment. This is accomplished by working through the meanings of termination.	Through T's ability to assist P in internalizing the gains.

Some of the theory's basic premises first need to be stated here:

Theory of Psychotherapeutic Change

1. The theory's concepts do not deal with the physical determinants of behaviors, but rather with their psychological representations in experience such as feelings, thoughts, perceptions, and memories.

2. The theory relies on a broad definition of experience, one not limited to conscious experience, for as Freud observed ([1915]1958), conscious experience is only a restricted and vacillating condition.

Question 1: What Changes?

The next three premises provide a framework within which to locate what it is that changes:

3. The theory covers both change and stability in behavior as multiply determined by the interaction of psychological, physical, biological, and cultural factors. This interaction has experiential representations within the individual's personality —the entity which is changing and is at the same time the intervening variable between external impacts and behavioral change. General and specific improvement in the main symptoms are the most obvious changes to take place in the personality; the symptoms most likely to improve are those that are related to the treatment goals.

4. Within the personality, it is the psychological conflicts that most require change.

5. During the sessions, it is the relationship problems that are the most accessible and therapeutically usable expression of these conflicts; they tend to be directly involved in the patient's suffering and therefore to require change. The conflicts expressed in the core conflictual relationship patterns are transference potentials; they are ready to be actualized in relation-

ship after relationship, like a theme and variations on a theme. Freud ([1912a]1958) has referred to the transference potentials as relationship "stereotype plates" since certain of their components get reproduced repeatedly in nearly identical versions, in spite of their self-hurtful nature. The patient's treatment goals reflect the desire to change some of these relationship components.

EXAMPLE: Ms. C. K.

An initial goal for Ms. C. K. before treatment was expressed by her main complaint: "I can't have a relationship with a guy." In her early sessions, her most prevalent relationship pattern as formulated in the core conflictual relationship theme (CCRT), was this: "I wish to be able to open up in relationships but I'm afraid to because I'll get rejected." In the beginning of treatment the part of the pattern she most wanted to change was the negative consequences of her wish, so that she would be able to "open up" without experiencing rejection and therefore be able to sustain a "relationship with a guy."

An additional premise presents another aspect of the limits of awareness:

6. The condition of being unaware of something is not just a passive condition but is actively perpetuated by resistances to awareness. Consequently, providing the patient with the missing information may not be sufficient in itself to fill in the gaps since the patient is defended against knowing some components of the CCRT or its associated themes because of attendant painful feelings that would be mobilized by such awareness.

Although Ms. C. K. was often aware of the main components of her CCRT, she was not aware of how central the theme was in determining her relationships. Only at times, and then only partially, was she aware of the similarity of her problem of being unable to open up in relationships with her mother's parallel problem. She showed no awareness of the associated relationship theme of her expectation of harm from her father in response to her impulse to open up to men, including her father. She could not have filled in the missing awareness by being presented with the information, unless she had also worked it through in the treatment.

The psychoanalytic theory makes frequent use of the concept of intrapsychic conflict. What is it which conflicts with what? As this example from Ms. C. K. (and those of other patients discussed in later chapters) imply, the structure of the conflictual relationship patterns are divisible, as in the following premise:

7. The CCRT theme is comprised of two classes of components which are often in conflict.

Class A: A wish, need, or intention. Psychoanalytic theorists tend to call these derivatives of id impulses. (For Ms. C. K. this wish is, "I wish to open up in relationships.")

Class B: A control or executive function with access to some information about the internal and external conditions which may be relevant to the expression and possible satisfaction of the wish, need, or intention. Psychoanalytic theorists tend to call class B functions a central property of the ego and its offshoot, the superego. The operation of class B determines the person's responses to the wish, need, or intention. These responses are classified in this scheme as responses from the object (RO) and responses from the self (RS). (For Ms. C. K. the RO is "I will be rejected and the RS is "I will withdraw.)

These two concepts involving the two classes of components that are often in conflict are appropriate, therefore, for describing the changes that come about through psychoanalytically oriented psychotherapies. Some research-based experiences already suggest these conclusions: (1) The CCRT tends to remain recognizable at and after termination, even for patients who have shown much general and specific improvement (Luborsky 1977; Pfeffer 1959). (2) Some kinds of changes in the CCRT do occur; however, these changes tend to be in the consequences, while the wish, need, or intention components change relatively little (Levine and Luborsky 1981). The changes that take place in the patients who have improved include the following: an increased understanding of some of the core conflictual relationship patterns; an increased mastery of some components; and the dropping and adding of some components. These changes in understanding might be termed by psychoanalytic theorists as "lifting of repressions" or by another metaphor which suggests both changes in understanding and in mastery, "where id was there shall ego be" (Freud [1932]1964).

What is the nature of the increase in mastery? After all, the increase implies that the original CCRT and the relationship problems in it remain recognizable at and after termination, even in patients who have improved. One answer can be expressed in spatial terms: the person has a different position in relation to the suffering-engendering relationship theme. A *New Yorker* cartoonist depicted this change in position in a way that is often appropriate to the meaning of increased mastery in psychotherapy. In the first cartoon of a sequence, a man is shown coming to a building for his psychotherapy session, pedaling his bike laboriously under the added strain of a monkey perched on his back. In the next illustration, he is shown after the psychotherapy session, riding away from it on his bicycle, with the monkey still present, but riding its own bicycle alongside his. The monkey is still there, but it is not so burdensome and is now in view.

8. The changes in mastery derive from more than the working out of the suffering-engendering relationship problems of the CCRT, such as occur on the level of a change from expected negative consequences to expected positive consequences. Once changes are achieved on this level they may then open the way to a better general level of functioning. The changes may be considered to have enabled the person to function at a higher level of organization, that is, at a higher developmental level (Greenspan 1981a and b; Greenspan and Polk 1980).

Question 2: How Does Change Come About?

The techniques derive, in a generally logical but loosely deduced fashion, from the theory of psychotherapeutic change. Three central curative factors are listed below in the order of their emphasis in the most authoritative statements of the theory, and will be discussed in relation to it. Although the theory is well known to be multifaceted, its many subordinate components comfortably cluster around these three main ones:

CURATIVE FACTORS

The first factor, self-understanding, is achieved through expressive techniques. To judge from the prominence given to it in clinical psychoanalytic writings, it is the most significant of the three. The second factor, the helping alliance, is achieved through supportive techniques, in collaboration with the patient's readiness to experience the alliance. The third factor, the incorporation of the gains so that they will remain with the

patient, is facilitated by attention to the meanings of termination. Since the patient and the therapist each make their own
special contribution to each of these three curative factors, each
factor has a patient component and a therapist component.

1. Achieving Understanding
*Patient Component: The patient's involvement in the process
of achieving understanding.*

The theory of psychotherapeutic change posits that the main
preliminary to the patient's improvement is an increase in
understanding. The focus of the understanding tends to be
around the present symptoms and the associated relationship
problems. The reexperiencing with the therapist in the "here
and now" of the conflictual relationship problems gives the
patient the most impetus toward meaningful insight and permits greater freedom to change. Past relationships gain in
meaning when they are related to the current ones. Keeping
the relevance of the present in sight is one way for the therapist
to insure that the insight is emotionally meaningful and not
just intellectual.

The insight becomes progressively more meaningful to the
patient as new editions of the relationship problems are repeatedly worked through with the therapist and others. As Freud
([1914] 1958) described, a major agenda of the patient is to
remember and to repeat the conflictual relationship problems
in the relationship with the therapist. The repetition can be
seen as being in the service of finding ways to master the
problems (Mayman 1978). The repetition also represents an
actualization of the patient's unconscious plan to revive the
relationship problems and to overcome them by testing the
present relationship with the therapist in terms that are appropriate for the participants in the early versions of the relationship problems (Weiss and Sampson 1984).

Theory of Psychotherapeutic Change

Working through the relationship problems by remembering and repeating them provides the patient with increased control and mastery. Such gains are shown by changes on two levels. First, the patient becomes able to think about aspects of the relationship problems with greater tolerance and comfort; the classical theory refers to the changes as lifting or undoing of repression. Second, on the level of action, the patient tends to find more adaptive ways of behaving, even though elements of the early relationship patterns tend to be still discernible, that is, the transference potentials remain recognizable.

Therapist Component: The therapist's ability to facilitate the patient's involvement in the process of achieving understanding.
This manual is a variation of a how-to-do-it guide; it is a how-to-help-the-patient-to-do-it guide. The therapist's job is to elicit the patient's ability also to do the job of achieving understanding. The understanding is about some facets of the current relationship problems and those aspects of the past ones that may have contributed to them. The psychoanalytically oriented therapist thinks of some of the current relationship problems of the patient as susceptible to involvement in the transference. Consequently, the therapist's expressive task is to engage the patient in a working through of edition after edition of the relationship problems as these are expressed in the transference. The concept of resistance is implicitly integrated into this presentation of the theory of technique. The patient's resistances are interpersonal behaviors through which the patient opposes the therapeutic efforts. Resistances therefore show themselves through transference, so that interpreting the transference is interpreting the resistance, as Gill (1982) cogently concludes.

The therapist's expressive task, in which the patient is also enlisted, is described in this manual as having four main phases. Phase 1, Listening: to listen with a high degree of openness to what the patient is saying; phase 2, Understanding: to attend during this listening to the understanding which will occur of the patient's main symptoms and sources of pain as well as to the theme of the associated relationship problems; phase 3, Responding: to impart this understanding to the patient at points which are tactfully timed, in amounts which are readily assimilable, and in ways which facilitate the working through process; and phase 1', Returning to listening: while taking into account the patient's response to what the therapist said. The last phase entails an interactive feedback system between the patient and the therapist. After the therapist attains sufficient understanding of the core conflictual relationship problems, and after presenting a facet of these to the patient, the patient's response provides the therapist with further understanding, some of which is then used in the therapist's further response, and so on. In this fashion the patient and therapist travel in tandem.

2. Achieving a Helping Relationship

Patient Component: The patient's ability to experience the relationship with the therapist as helpful.

The concept of the helping alliance has a long history going back to an aspect of Freud's views of the transference ([1912a] 1958). He distinguished two kinds of attachment: one which facilitates cooperation and the other which interferes with it. The cooperation-facilitating part is the "conscious," "unobjectionable," positive feelings of the patient to his or her therapist. This part forms one basis for the helping alliance experience and is like the first of the two broad types of helping alliances described in Luborsky (1976): type 1, in which the patient experiences the therapist as providing or being capable of providing the help which is needed and type 2, in which the patient experiences treatment as a process of working together with the therapist toward the goals of the treatment. It is type 2, more than type 1, which tends to be referred to when the concept is used in more recent clinical writings (Greenson 1967).

Therapist Component: The therapist's ability to facilitate the patient's experience of the relationship with the therapist and of the treatment as helpful.

Three powerful structural sources of facilitation of the helping alliance are brought about by the therapist: (1) The treatment circumstances of SE, along with all forms of psychotherapy, contain conditions that are inherently supportive. Among these are the regular meetings for the psychotherapy sessions and the therapist's tacit or explicit agreement to be helpful to the patient in attaining the patient's goals, as expressed by the the therapist's agreement to engage in the treatment. (2) The therapist's attitude of sympathetic understanding has a further positive effect in allowing the patient to develop a helping alliance (Freud [1913]1958). (3) The therapist may just happen to fit the patient's conception of a helpful person, one who can be trusted, relied upon, and loved (e.g., as shown even in the first session by Ms. E. S. who saw in the therapist similarities to the man she loved but was trying to stop seeing because he was married.)

Nevertheless, from time to time and with selected patients (chapter 6), the therapist finds it necessary to strengthen the helping alliance by the techniques given in this manual. These techniques are necessary, according to Wallerstein and Robbins (1956) and Schlesinger (1969), for either well-functioning people who are temporarily overwhelmed by a stressful problem or anxiety, or for more severely disturbed people with low anxiety tolerance and poor controls who require strengthening of their defenses (Gill 1951).

3. Incorporating the Gains

Patient Component: The patient's ability to internalize and therefore to hold the gains of treatment after its completion.

Loss of the gains after the treatment is over is a problem in any form of psychotherapy (Atthowe 1973). Psychoanalytically oriented psychotherapies have concepts to explain the erosion of or retention of the gains. A useful one is internalization, which is a process the patient uses to retain the gains of the psychotherapy, especially by incorporating the image of the therapist as a helpful person and by learning to use the therapist's stock-in-trade of treatment tools.

Internalization has a natural function in the maturation of most people, so natural that we take it for granted (Ekstein 1969). However, we readily recognize when it is absent, as in the contrast in behavior of two young boys who came to the edge of a swimming pool with the intention of jumping in. One jumped in without hesitation but the other could not. He asked the first one how he did it. The first explained "My parents told me it was okay and I saw others jump in. I can tell myself it will be okay. The water will stay there and buoy me up." The second one explained, "I was told that but I can't realize it. So I can't jump." The patient must be able to say to himself or herself, at least by the end phase of the treatment, that what has been learned during its course will remain, even though the schedule of face-to-face psychotherapy sessions will come to an end. However, what has been learned and the impression of the helping relationship will stay alive.

The retention of the gains is a usual benefit of such working through of the meanings of termination. Occasionally, however, that is not the case, as in this example: Among the patients in the Penn Psychotherapy Project (Luborsky, Mintz, Auerbach, Christoph, Bachrach, Todd, Johnson, Cohen, and

O'Brien 1980), there was one with an exceptional deficiency in ability to internalize (Mr. B. N. described in appendix 4). He had had three periods of psychotherapy, of which the last was part of the study. In each of these he made impressive gains, but then within about a year the gains always seriously eroded. It was difficult for him to maintain an internalized representation of the therapist, and he showed other qualities now popularly called "borderline" characteristics (Kernberg 1975). Like the boy who was unable to jump into the water he was unable to realize that he could stay afloat when he was no longer seeing the therapist.

Therapist Component: The therapist's ability to work through with the patient the meaning of termination in ways that help the patient to hold the gains of the treatment.

The therapist's task of helping the patient work through the meaning of termination is considered to be an essential part of the job of psychoanalytically oriented psychotherapy (Freud [1937] 1964) as well as of some other treatments, for example, Janis (1982). Various ways of implementing this curative factor are given in chapter 9, especially by recognizing the resurgence of symptoms as a way of dealing with the meaning of termination. The patient can also benefit by being helped to distinguish different types of feelings about the impending separation. Two common feelings that need to be differentiated are the natural sadness at facing the ending of the meetings with someone who has been helpful and to whom one has become attached, versus the concern about losing someone who is needed because the benefits of the treatment cannot be maintained without the continued contact. The patient may express the concern directly and/or by a reappearance of symptoms that had been overcome before the frightening meanings of the termination had begun to be felt. In whatever way the concern is communicated, the therapist may recognize it by a response of this sort: "You believe that the gains you have made are not part of you but depend on my presence. You fear that you will lose the gains when we stop our regular schedule of sessions and your initial symptoms will come back, as they have recently begun to in anticipation of termination." Such a response by the therapist tends to allay the concern and dissipate the revival of the symptoms so that the gains will once more be evident.

The Relative Power of Curative Factors 1 and 2: Achieving Understanding versus Achieving a Helpful Relationship

The pursuit of greater understanding is to be engaged in by the therapist with the realization that it cannot be of much use unless an adequately supportive relationship is present. The reminder is not intended to diminish the therapist's faith in the power of understanding; under proper conditions it has a value in its own right in helping the patient to gain mastery over the impairing conflicts. At the same time, the successful pursuit of understanding may also help to achieve the supportive relationship by providing a meaningful agenda for the joint work of the patient and therapist.

Even though the two curative factors work in tandem, when they are isolated for the sake of comparison, the power of the relationship may prove to be the more potent of the two. In historical perspective, this weighting should be no surprise. It has been known through the centuries that a relationship with another person who is seen as helpful can be curative, and the loss of such a relationship has also been known for its power in setting off psychic and somatic illness (Schmale 1958).

The Relative Curative Power of Treatment Factors versus Other Factors

An even broader view reveals the bounds of the treatment factors and their articulation with other classes of factors. Clearly, from this perspective, even with a skilled therapist's impeccable adherence to the SE treatment recommendations, such purity could not always produce the desired benefits for all patients because the treatment factors are but one class of change factors. As important as they are, they appear in general to be less crucial than the patient factors in influencing the outcomes of psychotherapy (Luborsky, Mintz, Auerbach, Crits-Christoph, Bachrach and Cohen, in press). Among the patient factors, one has especially strong evidence to support its importance: it is the patient's psychological health-sickness, or psychiatric severity. This factor cuts across diagnostic categories since it reflects the severity of the psychological symptoms, regardless of the type of disorder. It is this severity dimension which may hinder the patient from being able to use the treatment to best advantage.

In this chapter recognition has been given to three factors: the treatment, the therapist, and the patient. A fourth, and obvious, factor has been omitted: it is the patient's life situation. Although life situational factors are little discussed in this book, undoubtedly in some instances they can be pivotal in determining the outcome of the patient's treatment. It is a premise of the theory that the four factors do not operate in isolation. The changes are based on the interaction and balance of the factors, with the patient's personality as the intervening variable between external inputs from the life situation and changes in the patient.

3

Psychotherapy Manuals: A Small Revolution in Research and Practice

Readers will make better use of the manual format of this book if they understand how psychotherapy manuals developed from the late 1970s to the present day.

A Short History of Psychotherapy Manuals

During this period psychotherapy researchers have come to consider that good research designs require manuals with the three essential components: definitive statements of the psychotherapy principles; concrete guides to carrying out the techniques; and scales to estimate the degree to which the techniques were used. Such manuals are especially needed for studies that compare the relative effectiveness of different forms of psychotherapy.

Other advocates of such increased and improved psychotherapy research have included the third-party insurance payers, some congressional committees during the Carter administration, Gerald Klerman, former director of Alcohol, Drug Abuse and Mental Health Administration, and many research psychologists and psychiatrists. Over the past 15 years or so there has been a growing feeling that an attempt must be made to do for the psychotherapies what had been done for the pharmacotherapies, namely, to try to calibrate what and how much was being delivered, and then to find out how effective it was. After about 40 years of a steady stream of small studies comparing psychotherapies (as attested to by Luborsky, Singer, and Luborsky 1975; Smith, Glass, and Miller 1980, and others), this promised increase in research backing was welcomed. As reported in the American Psychological Association publication, *Monitor*, June 1980, "Senate Finance Health Subcommittee staff have been working with administration officials and professional groups, including the American Psychological Association and the American Psychiatric Association, in an effort to come up with a bill redefining eligible health providers under Medicare and Medicaid and to establish clinical trial studies of psychotherapy" (p. 1). Despite the talk of further fund cuts in the early to mid-1980s, the direction of the research appears to have been maintained, although without the earlier momentum.

The very first treatment manuals were designed for the classical behavior therapies (e.g., Wolpe 1969). The later advent of manuals for the psychodynamic psychotherapies can be understood in light of the fact that it is easier to design a manual for a prescriptive treatment than for a nonprescriptive one. The behavioral and other advice-giving treatments, such as behavior therapies, cognitive–behavioral therapy, and drug counseling, are easier for the manual writer to write since much of what is to be done by the therapist is known in advance. In a less prescriptive treatment, such as psychoanalytically oriented psychotherapy, much of what the therapist has to do must be tailor-made for the patient and the occasion, after the therapist has listened to and conceptualized the patient's problems.

The output of manuals has expanded geometrically so that there is a small boom looming in the manuals market. Because the research style that requires manuals was set so recently, some of the manuals have not yet been commercially published but have been duplicated and used in training and research programs. The dates they were first written and copyrighted show their recency. Psychotherapy manuals include the following: (1) those for psychoanalytically oriented psychotherapy: Luborsky (1976); (2) those for interpersonal psychotherapy: Klerman and Neu (1976); Klerman, Rounsaville, Chevron, Neu, and Weissman (1979); (3) those for cognitive-behavioral psychotherapy: Beck and Emery (1977); Beck, Rush, Shaw, and Emery (1978); (4) those for nonscheduled minimal treatment controls: Luborsky and Auerbach (1979) adapted from DiMascio, Klerman, Weissman, Prusoff, Neu, and Moore (1978); (5) for short-term dynamic psychotherapy: Strupp and Binder (1982); and (6) for six treatments for drug-dependent patients (Woody, Luborsky, and McLellan in preparation).

As further evidence of the precipitous rise in popularity of manuals, the American Psychiatric Association has appointed a commission on psychiatric therapies (APA Commission 1982) which is attempting to develop a psychiatric treatment manual. This ambitious project is an effort to define the characteristics of all of the psychiatric treatments and to identify their therapeutic effectiveness and the types of patients for whom they are best suited.

Some of these treatment manuals have been utilized in studies now completed or in progress (Weissman 1979; Neu,

Prusoff, and Klerman 1978). By far the largest and best-known study using manuals is the Depression Collaborative study (Waskow, Hadley, Parloff, and Autry 1979) which is comparing interpersonal psychotherapy, cognitive–behavioral psychotherapy, and psychopharmacotherapy. Although this study is still in progress it has already created an extraordinary effect by supporting the small revolution in research practice, and by firmly setting the pattern, begun previously, for comparative studies of psychological treatments to incorporate treatment manuals in their designs.

Research Findings Based on Non-Manual-Based Psychotherapies

The use of manuals to guide therapists in the conduct of psychotherapies should sharpen the distinctions which can be made by clinicians who are presented with samples of different psychotherapies. However, the ability of clinicians to identify manual-guided psychotherapies has hardly been studied at all, while non-manual-guided psychotherapies have been examined for two or three decades. The latter studies show that distinctions among treatments can usually be made and that these distinctions are generally consistent with the theory of the psychotherapy or some derivative of the theory. To cite a few examples: Strupp (1958) showed that the therapists in client-centered psychotherapy (Rogers 1957) relied primarily on summarizing the patient's feelings, whereas the therapists in short-term analytic therapy (Wolberg 1967) were more highly inferential. Auerbach (1963) compared Witaker and Malone's (1981) experiential therapy with Wolberg's (1967) short-term approach and found that Wolberg's used fewer interpretations, less direct guidance, and was less inferential. Bruninck and Schroeder (1979) showed similarities in empathy among Gestalt and behavior therapists but found differences in the use of direct guidance, facilitative techniques, therapist self-disclosure, therapist initiative, and supportive climate.

A comparison of psychoanalytically oriented psychotherapy and behavior therapy (Sloane, Staples, Christol, Yorkson, and Whipple 1975), showed the behavior therapists to be more active; they dominated the conversation more, speaking for a much higher proportion of the session, and making more information-providing statements to the patient than the psychotherapists. Unexpectedly, however, there were no differences between the two types of therapists in their use of statements interpreting and clarifying the patients' problems. Perhaps the categories in the study were too broadly defined to catch the differences that existed. Nevertheless, in general, the Sloane et al. study (1975) and others using speech pattern and other content analyses have found that the therapy sessions mostly were consistent with the basic characteristics of the intended treatment.

Research Findings Based on Manual-Based Psychotherapies

One of the earliest examinations of the techniques used in a manual-based psychotherapy was carried out for interpersonal psychotherapy of depression (Neu, Prusoff, and Klerman 1978). The aim in that study was to find and describe the techniques used by therapists who had been trained to follow the manual for interpersonal psychotherapy (IPT) by Klerman and Neu (1976). Over all sessions, these therapists used these components: nonjudgmental exploration 45 percent of the time, elicitation 21 percent, clarification 14 percent, and direct advice only 7 percent of the time. Their performance was in accord with IPT. As we will see below, the first three components of this manual-based treatment are also like SE psychotherapy while the direct advice component is more like CB psychotherapy.

A large study of substance abuse patients (Woody, McLellan, Luborsky, and O'Brien 1981) evaluated the ability of clinical judges to recognize samples of each of three manual-based therapies (Luborsky, Woody, McLellan, O'Brien, and Rosenzweig 1982). The therapies were: drug counseling (DC) (Woody, Stockdale, and Hargrove 1977); supportive–expressive psychotherapy (SE) (Luborsky 1976b); and cognitive–behavioral psychotherapy (CB) (Beck and Emery 1977). The rating forms used by the clinical judges contained scales for three or four specific criteria for each type of therapy and a global scale for the degree to which the treatment fit the specifications of each treatment manual (see appendix 3). Two independent judges rated scales for these criteria from 15-minute samples of each psychotherapy. Another independent judge counted the frequency within the same samples of a set of precise speech content categories (the Temple content categories in Sloane et al. 1975).

These results emerged from Luborsky et al. (1982):

1. The judges discriminated among the three treatments through listening to samples of the sessions. In the first substudy they recognized the intended form of therapy in 73 percent of the sessions, and in the second substudy in 80 percent of the sessions (chance levels of recognition would be 33 percent).

2. The two independent judges gave the same designation to each type of therapy an average of 67 percent of the time.

3. Each treatment was most distinctive on the single rated overall criterion; for example, "the degree to which the treatment fits the specifications of SE psychotherapy." The overall rating for the two independent judges for SE on a 5-point scale was 2.8 (which was significantly different from the ratings for DC and CB at less than the 0.01 level). Certain of the specific techniques recommended in the manual were more easily distinguished. The SE therapy was judged to be significantly more focused on "the understanding of the relationship with the patient including the transference." Also, the SE therapy had a greater degree of "focus on facilitating self-expression as part of the search for understanding." The CB therapy showed "directiveness" to be its most distinctive component, followed by "finding cognitive distortions" and "challenging cognitive beliefs." The DC therapy was most distinctive in "monitoring current problems as well as giving advice."

4. Certain qualities recommended in the manuals gave virtually identical mean ratings for three treatments; they were not significantly different from each other. The best example of this was "giving support": in all three treatments it received middle-level ratings which were not significantly different from each other. Consequently, it seems likely that, regardless of the form of treatment, providing support is a common feature of psychotherapies. Nevertheless, although it has a prominent place in the SE manual, by contrast, it has relatively little place in the CB and DC manuals. It seems justifiable to conclude, therefore, that what is presented explicitly in a given manual as curative may not, in fact, be representative of what is curative in a treatment.

A more comprehensive impression of the components of a treatment can be achieved by examining the profile of types of therapist's statements and comparing the profiles across differ-

TABLE 3.1.

Content Analysis of Psychotherapy: Percentage of Each Type of Therapist Statement.[e]

	Penn–VA Study[d]			Yale Study	Temple Study	
	DC	SE	CB	IPT[a]	"SE"[b]	B[c]
Number of Tapes	35	27	21	9	30	30
Content of Category						
Average % Time speaking	29.1	14.4	35.5	26.5	—	—
Asking for information statements	27.1	17.2	39.5	18.4	32.0	32.0
Giving information statements	17.4	2.6	3.5	1.6	3.0	7.0
Clarification and interpretation statements	8.2	13.0	21.3	20.9	26.0	32.0
Nondirective statements	35.6	62.3	24.9	47.1	44.0	26.0
Directive statements	4.2	1.7	5.8	5.9	2.0	8.0
Approval statements	3.4	2.4	3.6	1.7	1.0	2.0
Disapproval statements	4.1	0.7	1.4	4.3	0.5	1.0

Groups underlined are
not significantly different
within Penn-VA

[a]The Yale study *IPT* was interpersonal psychotherapy (Data kindly provided by B. Rounsaville.)
[b]The Temple study *SE* was psychoanalytically oriented psychotherapy (Sloane et al. 1975).
[c]The Temple study *B* was behavior therapy.
[d]The Penn–VA study *DC* was drug counseling, *SE* was the supportive-expressive psychotherapy discussed in this manual, and the *CB* was cognitive–behavioral psychotherapy.
[e]These percentages add up to 100 when "percentage time speaking" is excluded. The Temple study percentages are not exact since they were estimated from a graph (in Sloane et al. 1975, Figure 25, p. 159); the data themselves had been destroyed.

ent treatments. Some of this is presented in table 3.1 for data from the Penn-VA study (Woody et al. 1981), the Yale study (Rounsaville, Glazer, Wilber, Weissman, and Kleber, 1983), and the Temple study (Sloane et al 1975). (The Penn and Yale data were scored independently by one judge) By inspection it is clear that the most distinctive profile among those compared is the one for DC therapy. The IPT tends to fall between the SE and CB profiles. The SE psychotherapy represented in the

37

Temple study seems to have characteristics in common with the SE of the Penn-VA study.

5. Certain objectively counted content categories, from the Temple Content Category Method (Sloane et al. 1975) showed significant differences among treatments. Some outstanding examples (from substudy 2) follow:

The "therapists' percentage of time speaking" was 14 percent for SE, 36 percent for CB, and 29 percent for DC. When the SE therapists did speak, their comments were more "nondirective": SE 62 percent, CB 25 percent, and DC 36 percent. (The counterparts of these therapist techniques are found in the patient's behavior; for example SE patients spoke 79 percent of the time while the CB patients spoke 53 percent, and the DC patients 57 percent of the time.) When just three of the therapists' content categories are taken together, a remarkable degree of discrimination among the therapies appears. The three are "the percent nondirective statements," "the percent clarification statements and interpretation," and "the percent questions." A discriminant function yielded correct classification of 100 percent of the CB tapes, 95 percent of the SE tapes, and 91 percent of the DC tapes. It is amazing that just three objectively counted bits of therapist behavior could make so clear a distinction among the three treatments. Moreover, it is noteworthy that although these three content categories are not explicitly stipulated by the manual, they are consistent with the spirit of the manual. For example, the SE manual does not instruct the therapists to minimize speaking, although SE therapists would be expected to speak less than CB and DC therapists.

One other study investigated the discriminability of samples of different types of psychotherapy and found similar results (DeRubeis, Hollon, Evans, and Bemis 1982). The two forms of therapy, CB and IPT, were both used for the treatment of depression. For each of the two treatments, six videotapes were judged by 12 raters. Each rater listened to and/or viewed four tapes, two from each of the two types of treatment. The ratings of each tape were on a 48-item Likert-type rating scale, the Minnesota Tape Rating Scale. The raters were also asked to judge the "good, typical" CB or IPT therapy session using the same scale.

The results show successful discrimination of the two types of psychotherapy: 38 of the 48 items were discriminated, usually in the direction of the differences observed by the experts' predictions, with four principal factors accounting for 69 percent of the variance. Factor 1 is CB technique, factor 2 is general therapeutic skills, factor 3 is therapist directiveness, and factor 4 is IPT technique.

By training therapists to use manuals and then rating them on manual-based categories, it is possible to measure what is actually delivered, both by each type of treatment and by each therapist providing each treatment. Along these lines McLellan has noted (unpublished data) that therapists differ in the degree to which they provide the techniques from their own manual and do not provide those from other manuals. A ratio of the use of techniques from the therapist's own manual versus all techniques used provides an estimate of each therapist's "purity of technique." Furthermore, findings suggest that the therapists with the greatest purity of technique have the best treatment outcomes (Luborsky, McLellan, Woody, O'Brien and Auerbach in press). This type of result is further supported by the finding that even within the caseload of each therapist, the relationship holds—the patients of each therapist who delivered the purest treatment improved the most.

Apparently the more a treatment is carried out according to what is intended by its treatment manual, the more effective is the treatment and the better the outcome. Another, not necessarily exclusive possibility is that when patients are improving, the therapists are most able to carry out their intended techniques.

However, the design of the Penn-VA Psychotherapy Study on the recognizability of manual-based psychotherapies does not permit a definite conclusion about whether this considerable degree of recognizability of the therapies and their discrimination by objectively counted codes is really a function of having used manuals to guide the therapists. To answer that question, a research design is needed in which the therapist's conformity to the manual's treatment techniques is compared for manual-guided treatment versus non-manual-guided treatment. That should be the subject of a new study.

Future Research Applications

The contributions of manuals in psychotherapy research are likely to serve three main purposes by providing for:

1. More Objective Comparisons of Psychotherapies in Research Studies. The categories in the manual can serve as a basis for rating the techniques employed in each treatment. These ratings can then reveal the ways in which psychotherapies are distinct from each other or overlap (as illustrated in Luborsky et al. 1982; DeRubeis et al. 1982).

2. More Precise Measurement of the Degree to Which Each Therapist Provided What Was Recommended in the Manual. Rating Scales developed from the manual can be used to estimate the degree to which the intended form of psychotherapy described in the manual was actually provided. In this way the degree of conformity by each therapist to the intended form of treatment as described in the manual can be measured. A related investigation is under way on the degree to which the therapist's conformity to the specifications of the manual predicts the outcomes of the psychotherapy (Luborsky, McLellan Woody, O'Brien and Auerbach in press). The level of conformity may reflect the therapist's ability to carry out the recommendations in the manual and, therefore, reflect the therapist's skill.

3. More Facilitation of the Training of Therapists in the Specific Form of Psychotherapy. Since the treatment manuals specify the main techniques of a psychotherapy, they provide guides for training psychotherapists, both for clinical practice and for participation in research studies. Furthermore, the usefulness of the manuals in training can itself be investigated by scoring samples of the psychotherapy to see the degree to which conformity with recommendations in the manual gradually increases with training in its use.

4

How to Use the Manual

The methods for learning to use this manual are based on the tried and tested thesis of learning by doing. The "doing" involves these activities:

1. Read the manual, treat patients, and then reread.
2. Pursue training with a supervisor who refers to the relevant parts of the manual during the supervision.
3. Engage during the supervision in reviews of patient-therapist interactions by process notes, tape recordings, and role-playing.
4. Explore, jointly with the supervisor, the therapist's personality when it may be implicated in impediments to the therapist's performance.
5. Arrange for the therapist to have experience as a supervisor as a way to more firmly incorporate what has been learned.

Learning the Manual

The clinician who is ready to learn to use this SE manual, whether for practice or for research, should follow these alternating phases:

1. Read the manual.
2. Treat some patients while trying to apply it.
3. Read the manual again.
4. Treat some more patients while trying to apply it.
5. Check the conformity with the manual with a fellow therapist or supervisor.
6. And so on, until a reasonable level of mastery has been achieved.

This alternation of reading and practicing is a way to assimilate more fully what is in the manual; it is a way to get on to what is central in it. It minimizes drifting away from conformity to the manual: more drift tends to occur with a longer interval since the manual was last studied.

Concurrent Supervision

Learning supportive-expressive psychotherapy is best done by an apprentice method. That conclusion was the overwhelming consensus of those who had gone through such training. It was the retrospective verdict of several hundred psychiatric residents who were trained at the Menninger Foundation during the years 1946–1954 (Holt and Luborsky 1958). In a followup questionnaire they were asked what kinds of training experiences meant the most to them later on in developing their treatment style. Almost all responded that the psychotherapy supervision was far ahead of the usual lectures, case conferences, and reading. In terms of its impact on practice, it ranked along with the personal analysis.

But why use a manual at all for improving one's skill in psychotherapy? The most obvious reason is that for many people it is easier to learn the skills of a therapist when they read an integrated account of the psychotherapy rather than when they rely on the supervision alone. That is the testimony of many therapists who have tried this manual.

The manual is best assimilated when the learning occurs during individual supervision given by someone who is an expert on the SE manual, with the manual used as an adjunct to the supervision. Group supervision can be as helpful when the therapist is the presenter. Why is concurrent supervision so much more helpful than just reading the manual? Because of these four factors: (1) the supervisor can explain and illustrate the manual; (2) the relationship with the supervisor can be supportive to the therapist in overcoming anxiety about learning and about doing the therapeutic job (much as a therapist functions in relation to a patient); (3) the relationship of the supervisor and therapist may elicit from the therapist some parallel aspects of the therapist's relationship with the patient. Becoming aware of this parallel can at times be helpful in the supervision in understanding the therapist's relationship problem with the patient, as Ekstein and Wallerstein (1958) have illustrated in the standard guide on supervision methods; (4) the supervision sessions provide some opportunities for modeling the procedures recommended in the manual.

SUPERVISION PROCEDURES

The therapist should be introduced to the procedures of the supervisory sessions by the supervisor in these ways:

Choice of Patients. "In each of our sessions we will discuss at most only two patients, usually we will discuss just one. This concentration will help us come to know them very well. The choices of patients are up to you; you decide on the basis of your interests which ones to present."

Review of the Case Summary. "At the first session, you should bring a case summary of each patient you have chosen with a copy for me so I will have some information on the patient's background and diagnostic evaluation. We will discuss that in our first session especially and not much thereafter."

Review of Past Sessions. "Much more information of the kind we need for our discussions emerges from the sessions with the patient than from a case summary. In each of our sessions you will begin with a few minutes of review of what we have discussed before about the treatment in the last supervisory session."

Presentation of the Process Notes of the Intervening Sessions. "After the review you will present your process notes. A two or three page note on each session is usually adequate. We may only have time for the most recent one. The notes should contain some samples of what the patient said and some of what you said in response. The temporal sequence should be maintained to help us tune in to the flow of patient's communications in the session. In addition to giving samples of your interactions with the patient, it should give a general sketch of the session. The notes may be written just after the session is completed. Some therapists find that it does not interfere with their attention to make some notes during the session; others find it distracting. You must decide that on the basis of your own experience."

Comparison of Supervisor's and Therapist's Views. "Finally, you and I will compare notes about what we hear about the patient's main communications to you and your responses to them."

"In summary, in each of our sessions we will review the past sessions, listen to your process notes, and then make a new review of the patient's main communications and your responses to them."

Tape Recordings. "It is useful to record a sample of the sessions or all of the sessions even though only parts of them might be used for the supervision. As an aid to the supervision you can occasionally play brief excerpts from the tape recordings. Long replays of the tape would fill up too much of the time we have for the supervision. Very brief samples are sufficient to give a sense of the tone of the interaction of the patient and therapist. Then, when the usual process notes are presented, it will be possible for me (or the group) to be able to imagine how the patient and therapist sound by 'dubbing in the sound' from memory. Otherwise, process notes are usually preferable to recordings since they give a more rapid overview of the therapy."

Role Playing. The therapist and supervisor can profit at times from role playing and they often enjoy the enactments in which they model the patient and therapist responding to each other. The modeling may take this form: in the supervision sessions, after the therapist presents samples of process notes or brief samples of recordings of the treatment, the therapist and supervisor can take turns doing the kind of listening, understanding, and responding that is recommended for treating the patient. The exchange with the patient can be role-played with the therapist and supervisor alternating playing the part of patient and therapist and trying out anticipated dialogues (as was so memorably done in group supervision by Dr. Karl Menninger).

The times that role playing produces the most profit are those in which the therapist and the supervisor recognize the therapist's discomfort about dealing with the patient and/or that the therapist is overlooking an issue. The role playing can offer the therapist a sense of greater preparedness for the future dialogues with the patient by greater comfort and greater awareness of the issue that has not been understood.

EXAMPLE: Mrs. T.

The therapist was clearly in distress about his way of dealing with the patient's main message in the recent sessions. The message was (in essence): "I'm starved for affection and recognition of my interests, from you especially. If I don't get it I will be hurt. Then I will go out and get it directly sexually and in a way that is hurtful to me." The therapist explained to the supervisor the bind he felt he was in, that he was anxious about his ability to deal with this issue: "I feel if I acknowledge it she will want a directly gratifying response from me which I can't give and she will be even more upset."

Role-playing began with some of what the patient actually had said and led to some responses the therapist could make. The therapist gained confidence that he could be helpful to the patient through saying that he understood what she wanted from him and others. He could be helpful also by saying how hard it has been until now for her to have a relationship where her basic wish could be acknowledged. Until now she had felt that she had to be denied that experience in relationships and instead she had to express what she wanted in ways which made her guilty and were self-hurting.

THE THERAPIST'S PERSONALITY AS A FACTOR IN THE TRAINING

The typical discussion in the supervision session is directed toward identifying the patient's message in the session and the ways the therapist responded or did not respond to it. It is generally not necessary to go beyond this by observations about the therapist's personality. Sometimes, however, the therapist's personality interferes with the relationship with the patient or with the supervisor. In fact there is often a parallel between the patient-therapist interaction and the supervisor-supervisee interaction which is helpful to notice, as described by Ekstein and Wallerstein (1958). It then becomes necessary to comment on the therapist's personality. The principle for the supervisor to follow is to introduce an observation about the therapist's personality only when recurrent interference has occurred with the therapist's being able to hear or being able to respond effectively to the patient's message.

EXAMPLE: (from the example of the supervision of Dr. Q.W.; P: Mrs. T.)

These are some examples of the supervisor's opening comments about the therapist's personality: "I note that the ideas we go over in supervision each week do not get reflected in what you do with the patient" etc. or "I notice that you usually miss a certain kind of message from this patient. The type of missed message is . . . " etc. Then the therapist's response to this general comment usually provides the material which determines the supervisor's next and more specific comment about the therapist.

THE THERAPIST AS SELF-SUPERVISOR AND PRACTICE SUPERVISOR OF OTHER THERAPISTS

The therapist generally keeps in mind the current state of the patient as it develops during the treatment but at times the therapist loses track of it and needs reminders. These can be provided most readily through the therapist's self-supervision, by a mental review or by a review of the process notes, especially the brief essences of the process notes. Sometimes the therapist may listen to sections of the tape recordings (as suggested by Rogers 1957b), although this is a very time consuming procedure.

Learning to do self-supervision can be helped by engaging in practice teaching. Instead of only the supervisor doing the teaching, the therapist should be enlisted to do the same job. In the supervision session the therapist, after presenting samples of the sessions, routinely goes on to review the essence of the patient's message and the therapist's responses. The supervisor does the same and then they compare their views. Later, after the therapist and supervisor decide that the therapist has a good grasp of the SE therapeutic system, opportunities should be found for the therapist to do some supervision with other therapists. If the form of supervision is group supervision, on the occasions when the supervisor is away, each member can rotate in the role of supervisor or the group can continue without a designated group leader. Such supervision experience helps to incorporate the learning and elevate it to an accessible-when-needed capacity for self-supervision.

Match Making

Much can be accomplished before the treatment starts by readying the patient for the opportunity. The way this is done can have a significant effect on its outcome. Proper preparation consists mostly of setting up appropriately positive and reasonably correct expectations about what the treatment will be like and arranging conditions for the most beneficial match of the patient and therapist. Some recommendations for doing this follow.

PREPARING THE PATIENT

Some initial preparation of the patient for psychotherapy is usually done by the referring doctor or a referring friend of the patient. The way in which these referring agents introduce therapy to the patient influences his or her expectations and may, at the very least, influence the patient's early response to the treatment. Naturally, when a trusted referring agent makes a positive recommendation of a particular therapist, treatment, or clinic, then the patient's expectations tend to be more positive. Further positive or negative expectations are stimulated by the interest and competence of the person who deals with the patient's initial inquiry about treatment and who makes the treatment arrangements.

The patient should be seen as soon as possible. Setting an appointment within a week or two of the initial contact means that the patient will start at the point of greatest readiness for treatment. A greater interval between initial contact and appointment can mean that the patient may lose the state of readiness, and this can lead to a higher proportion of unready or difficult-to-treat patients.

A PRELIMINARY SOCIALIZATION INTERVIEW

In short-term psychotherapy, special preparation of the patient for treatment can be crucial to its outcome. Just before the treatment starts, the therapist, or in the case of a clinic, a specially trained person should review with the patient the nature of the treatment to be started and encourage appropriate expectations about both treatment and therapist. In clinic settings this is best done by someone other than the therapist who has experience doing this interview and who can readily be seen by the patient as someone who is knowledgeable about the treatments offered at the clinic. In private practice it is equally desirable to have such preparation but it is not likely to be easily arranged. It might be carried out by a few usual referral sources.

Such "preliminary socializations" have been reported to have positive effects on the treatment, particularly for short-term treatments and for unsophisticated patients (Orne and Wender 1968; Goldstein and Simonson 1971). The positive effects are implied by Goldstein and Simonson (1971), who found that the patient who is more highly attracted to his or her therapist is in turn judged by the therapist to be more attractive. "When patient attraction to the therapist is high, the patient (1) is less covertly resistant, (2) talks more, (3) is self-descriptively sicker, (4) has more favorable prognostic expectancies for himself" (p. 164).

A recommended form of the preliminary socialization interview is the one by Orne and Wender (1968), samples of which are given in appendix 3. In the course of this form of preparatory interview the patient is told how the psychotherapy is conducted, what the patient is to do, and what the therapist is to do. A controlled comparison of patients who received the Orne and Wender interview versus those who did not, showed a significant advantage in their outcomes for those who had been prepared by these interviews (Hoehn-Saric, Frank, Imber, Nash, Stone, and Battle 1964; Nash, Hoehn-Saric, Battle, Stone, Imber, and Frank 1965).

SELECTING THE THERAPIST

In private practice, the therapist selection is made by the patient, who has, in most cases, been referred by a third-party. In a clinic, however, the selection of a therapist is typically made by a clinic agent, often a social worker. The selection decision tends to be based on which therapist has free time. Such assignments, therefore, allow the therapist relatively little expression of preference.

Research has not shown thus far which patient–therapist characteristics are reliable bases for fostering optimal matches; the same is true in terms of arranging matches of types of patients with types of treatments (Berzins 1977; Luborsky and McLellan 1981). Although some principles have been found in a few studies, they do not usually hold up under cross-validation. However, three types of research that offer more trustworthy leads, will be mentioned.

One type involves listening to both the patient's and the therapist's preference for each other based on information which gives each of them the opportunity to make an informed choice. The reward for attending to preferences is the making of a match that is less likely to burn out after a flash of promise. If any system is used beyond the mere filling of therapist time with the next patient, it is likely to be one based on judgments by an administrator. Sometimes these judgments are aided by test and interview assessments of patient and therapist. Rarely are the preferences of patient and therapist taken into account.

The participants' preference approach worked successfully in the Penn Psychotherapy Study (Luborsky, Mintz, Auerbach, Christoph, Bachrach, Todd, Johnson, Cohen, and O'Brien 1980). Here, half the therapists were allowed to choose the patients they preferred after a review of the patients' charts, while the other half of the therapists received randomly assigned patients. Having a choice versus not having a choice had a significant relationship to the benefits or lack of benefits their patients received. In addition, allowing the patient to express a preference, and even trying to find mutually agreeable matches between patient and therapist based on their preferences, is probably beneficial and needs to be tried in research studies (Luborsky and McLellan 1981).

Another type of study on the process by which patients and

therapists form a preference is in progress (Alexander, Luborsky, Auerbach, Cohen, Ratner, and Schreiber in preparation). This study is based on the Patient–Therapist Re-Pairing Opportunity Program of the Psychiatric Outpatient Clinic of the Hospital of the University of Pennsylvania. All participating patients who enter the program must first agree that they will have two sessions with one therapist, after which they will be interviewed about their response to that therapist. They will then have two sessions with another therapist after which they will be interviewed again about their response to the second therapist. Only then, at the end of the fourth session will they be allowed to make a choice about which of the two therapists they will continue with in treatment. Preliminary results indicate that most patients have a special preference for therapists with whom they believe they have or can establish a helping alliance, for whom they have a special liking, and with whom they believe they share important similarities.

Another lead, which may put us on a better path toward finding patient–treatment and patient-therapist matches, is provided by a study matching patients with six substance abuse treatment programs (McLellan, Luborsky, Woody, O'Brien, and Druley 1983). In that study, a good direction was found by taking into account the patient's psychiatric severity, since it was noted that the high severity group benefited little in all six treatment programs; at the other end of the scale, the low psychiatric severity group benefited much in all programs. Therefore, it seemed sensible to exclude the high and low severity groups and then to explore patient-treatment matches within the middle group only. When this was done a variety of relatively clear matches between patient and program appeared. Some cross-validation evidence is already available supporting this research strategy for finding matches (McLellan et al. 1983).

SELECTING THE PATIENT

As noted earlier, it is beneficial to arrange for patient and therapist to express their preferences for each other. Some patients who come to SE psychotherapy in a clinic setting have been told about various clinics and even about some therapists and in that way they can have some share in the selection process. A few actually shop around on their own among therapists in practice, and they have the most chance to express their preference.

The psychotherapy research literature does not contain specific guidelines as to which patients do best in SE psychotherapy versus other forms of psychotherapy (Luborsky, Singer, and Luborsky 1975). However, there is a growing body of psychotherapy research findings in which it has been shown that patient qualities are directly associated with good outcomes in psychotherapies in general (Luborsky, Mintz, Auerbach, Crits-Christoph, Bachrach, and Cohen in press). The outstanding patient quality that foretells greater benefits from psychotherapy is psychological health, the opposite of which is termed psychiatric severity.

One of the earliest studies of this was the Menninger Psychotherapy Project which revealed that patients who start psychotherapy psychologically healthier benefit more from treatment (Luborsky 1962). This is a quality having to do with the patient's psychological endowments and the individual's freedom from severe psychiatric symptoms. In economic terms, the principle could be referred to as "the rich get richer." In the extensive review of predictive psychotherapy studies, undertaken by the Penn Psychotherapy Project, 68 studies were located in which psychological health–sickness was tried as a predictor. Of these, 48 showed significant levels of prediction. The following are a sample of the predictive correlations in the main multivariate predictive studies: In the Penn Psychotherapy Project (Luborsky et al. 1980) psychological health-sickness correlated with one outcome measure (residual gain) .30* and with another outcome measure (rated benefits) 25*. We reanalyzed similar data from the Chicago Counseling Center Study (Fiske, Cartwright, and Kirtner 1964) and found similar significant predictors based on adequacy of psychological functioning. The Menninger Psychotherapy Project (Kernberg, Burstein, Coyne, Applebaum, Horwitz, and Voth 1972), the Temple University Project (Sloane, Staples, Cristol et al. 1975), and a Yale study (Rounsaville, Weissman, and Prusoff 1981), each showed some successful outcome predictions for psychological health–sickness measures at about the same significant but modest level as the Penn Psychotherapy Project.

Not only was psychological health–sickness predictive in psychotherapy studies, but it was also predictive in a variety of other treatments. In the study of six treatment programs for 800 substance abuse patients (McLellan et al. 1983), psychological severity provided significant prediction in the whole sample, as well as within each of the six programs (.34**). Of special interest in that study was the fact that the level of prediction happens to be better for psychological severity than for drug severity or any other kind of severity. In other words, the outcomes of drug abuse treatment can be predicted better from psychological health–sickness than from the severity of the drug abuse itself!

Some types of patient predictors were significant in other psychotherapy studies, but only a few of these were replicated and, therefore, they require more cross-validation. For example, in the Penn Psychotherapy Project (Luborsky et al. 1980),

* $= p < .05$
** $= p < .01$

"emotional freedom" (a composite of the variables, emotional freedom, initiative, flexibility, and optimistic expectation) correlated .30** with rated benefits, and a composite of 10 basic background and attitudinal similarities between patient and therapist correlated .24* with the main outcome measures (the three most significant similarities were age, marital status, and type of occupation).

Yet, no matter how a patient has been selected, SE has considerable flexibility to deal with many kinds of patients, being adaptable to a broad range of problems from mild situational maladjustments to borderline psychotic. The therapist deals with this broad range of severity by drawing on appropriate proportions of supportiveness versus expressiveness. As described in chapter 6, the greater the psychiatric severity, the more supportive and less expressive the therapy needs to be. It is partly this freedom to follow the principle of appropriate proportions of supportiveness versus expressiveness that makes SE more suitable than classical psychoanalysis for patients who are severely ill. This time-honored view has the support of clinical and research experience with these treatments (Wallerstein 1984).

The following is a summary of the research findings on which patients are judged to be most suitable for various psychotherapies:

1. Psychiatric severity is the most consistent predictor of outcome, not only in SE psychotherapy, but also in a variety of psychotherapies and other treatments.
2. Emotional freedom also tends to be predictive, possibly because of the motivational component contained in "optimistic expectations."

* = $p < .05$
** = $p < .01$

3. Basic demographic and attitudinal similarities between patient and therapist, particularly as to age, marital status, and type of occupation are also promising predictors.

Beyond the issue of suitability for psychotherapy, more research needs to be done to determine whether there are some qualities that make a patient especially suitable for one form of psychotherapy or another.

PART II

The Manual

5

Beginning Treatment

The opening and closing "moves" of psychotherapy, as Freud (1913) suggested in his chess game analogy, are clearer than the intervening ones. The recommended openings for the early sessions of the treatment follow. The therapist should:

1. listen in order to establish what the patient's problems are and let the patient try to cast these in terms of goals ordered in importance,
2. explain and demonstrate to the patient what the therapist does,
3. make explicit arrangements about the treatment,
4. allow a relationship of trust and rapport to be developed,
5. begin the process of formulating the basis for the main relationship problems and associated symptoms.

Setting Goals

The patient's goals are central to the therapeutic work. They bring the patient to therapy because they specify the desired changes. They also keep the patient coming to treatment and trying to change. It is a venerable observation that goals provide the motivation for change. Freud (1913, page 143) stated: "The primary motive force in the therapy is the patient's suffering and wish to be cured that arises from it." In terms of the theory of therapeutic change, the achievement of the goals is part of the interaction of the patient's working toward the goals, the capacity to change, and the adequacy of the two kinds of facilitating treatment conditions, supportiveness and expressiveness. The supportive relationship with the therapist especially serves as a sustaining impetus to change.

ELICITING GOALS

At some point in the first session the therapist may say, if the patient does not, "Tell me about the problems you wish to work on." Goal setting begins in the first session but recurs throughout the treatment as the patient comes to see the goals in a new light. Among the most common goals for many patients are the control of anxiety, depression, and problems of personal functioning. Whatever the goals, they should be set so that they take into account what seems achievable.

MONITORING PROGRESS BY REFERENCE TO GOALS

One of the functions of the initial setting of goals in SE psychotherapy is to make clear to both patient and therapist the ends toward which the treatment efforts will be directed. The setting of goals can offer a useful focus not only at the beginning but also throughout the process of treatment. In short-term time-limited SE psychotherapy especially, the luxury of a relaxed attitude toward time cannot be afforded and the focus on goals may speed the therapeutic work.

Goals provide markers of progress, or lack of it. After the treatment has been under way it can be valuable for the supervisor and the therapist from time to time to look back at the initial evaluation and first sessions to remind themselves of the patient's present position in relation to the initial goals. The most natural time for this retrospection is when a goal has been achieved. As Schlesinger (1977) has observed, when a goal is fulfilled, there will most likely be "internal markers" which signal the change so that there are ways of recognizing phases during the course of the treatment. These phases allow the patient and therapist to have a sense of completion and accomplishment along the way.

In addition, goal setting serves as a modulator or brake on regression. The absence of goal setting is counter-therapeutic for some patients because the lack of clear goals allows them to be susceptible to states, such as suspiciousness and dependency, which they cannot tolerate (as is demonstrated in the long example in chapter 6).

Explaining the Treatment Process

Besides reviewing the patient's goals, the therapist must explain and demonstrate what the patient and therapist will be doing. The therapist's explanation about the treatment process should be brief at this point because the patient will soon experience the treatment process and see what the therapist is doing. Lengthy explanations are unnecessary and may confuse the patient who can simply be instructed to talk about what he or she wishes to say. Then, as things become better understood, they will work together to figure out how to deal with what it is that impedes the patient from achieving goals and will collaborate in searching for ways of dealing with the patient's problems.

In SE psychotherapy the instruction that the patient should try to say what he or she is thinking is preferable to the instruction that the patient must say everything, as is recommended for classical psychoanalysis. To make saying everything that comes to mind a requirement can sometimes unnecessarily complicate the relationship with the therapist and it is not really necessary to make it a rule. The patient will come to realize that it is valuable to try to say what he or she is thinking since there will be opportunities to understand the basis for not having said things.

All patients fall silent sometimes and seem to not know what to say. They may explain that they do not know what to talk about. It will eventually become clear to them that thinking continues but speaking does not—that silences involve making decisions about what is or is not worth talking about. Realization by the patient and therapist of the basis for decisions to speak or not to speak can be helpful to the patient in working out the patient's problems (Freud 1913, pp. 137–138).

Making Arrangements for the Treatment

The main treatment arrangements that need to be settled at the beginning of treatment are (1) length of each session, (2) amount of the fee, (3) when the patient will be billed, (4) how much time the patient will have to pay the bill, (5) how missed sessions will be handled, (6) agreement about the appointment times, and (7) an estimate of the length of treatment. These are some recommended arrangements and principles for making them:

1. Length of each session: The usual length of a session is 50 minutes. It is desirable to let the patient know this at the outset and for the patient and therapist to adhere to it.

2. Amount of the fee: First the therapist should inquire about the patient's financial circumstances if they are not known and if the therapist has any leeway in fee setting. The therapist then tells the fee per session.

3. Patient billing: The patient should be told either: "The sessions will be billed at the end of each month," or, "Payment is to be made at each session."

4. When payment is due: The patient should be told that the bill is to be paid within a set time, such as two weeks after it is received.

5. Handling missed sessions: The therapist should make an arrangement at the start of treatment for handling missed sessions. These are two usual arrangements: "Any sessions you have to miss must be paid for since I will have reserved an hour and cannot fill missed hours," or "I will have to charge for the hour unless I am notified one (or two) days in advance."

The arrangement which is fairest to the therapist is to charge for all missed appointments by the patient since the patient is "leasing a definite hour" (Freud 1913:126). It is not possible in psychotherapy practice to fill missed sessions with sessions of other patients. This is true for therapists who do psychotherapy primarily as well as for those who only see a fixed number of patients per week in psychotherapy. However, in circumstances where the patient develops an organic illness or a major external event intervenes that prevents the patient from coming to the treatment for a period of time, the treatment can be considered terminated for the interim with the therapist being free to fill the sessions. When the patient is able to resume, the therapist can then take the patient back into treatment as soon as a free hour is available.

6. The appointment times: It is best to arrange a consistent hour each week although on some occasions it might be changed. When changes are made it is best to move them within the same week and then return to the usual meeting time.

7. The length of the treatment: Usually before the first treatment session the therapist will know which of the two time structures he will be using, the time-open-ended or time-limited (TL) arrangement. If it is the more usual open-ended arrangement, the therapist might say: "The treatment will go on until you and I come to a point where we agree a good time for termination has arrived."

In the first or second session when arrangements are being made for the time-open-ended treatment it is useful to add, "termination will come about when some of the goals you wish to achieve have been achieved." It is important for the therapist to make a further recommendation at this time early in the treatment: "However, at any time when termination is being considered for whatever reason, we should allow ourselves two or three sessions, at least, to review what we have done before the actual date of termination."

The patient has a right to have as clear an idea of the treatment length as the therapist is able to provide. The therapist routinely should explain that the range of treatment lengths is very wide. Some treatments may go on for several months and some may go on for several years. The length depends on the goals that are set and the pace at which the patient achieves them. The advantage of this time open-ended treatment structure is that it can be expanded or contracted in relation to the patient's needs.

SE-TL therapy is suited to the needs of some patients, clinics, and research programs where a brief, finite treatment length is convenient. For some patients it even serves as a further impetus to achieving the necessary changes because of its time limits. A recommended length for short-term treatment is between 12 and 25 sessions. One variation is a treatment length of 12 sessions spread over 16 weeks—the first sessions are scheduled weekly and the last ones bi-weekly. The therapist should say when it is fitting, that the time-limited arrangement can be helpful. If the patient is insecure about the treatment length and asks, "What if I need further treatment?" the therapist might say, "At that time we'll see how it goes for a while without treatment, and then review the possibility of referring you for further treatment if that is necessary."

Establishing a Relationship of Trust and Rapport

From the very beginning and throughout the treatment, establishing a good working relationship is of primary importance. The relationship ordinarily will get off to a good start just in the course of the therapist's doing the job of finding out the patient's goals and explaining how the treatment will proceed. The patient typically will be trying to judge whether the therapist is a reliable person, can be of help, and wants to be of help.

The concern with proper technique sometimes is unnecessarily responsible for the therapist's restraining his interest and inhibiting conformity with the usual social amenities. Samuel Lipton (1973) comments about this in a review of Blanton's recollections (1971) of his analysis with Freud: ". . . It (Blanton's book) is a moving testament to the unfailing interest and courtesy that Freud demonstrated in the teeth of the personal disasters of his last years. . . . It is quite clear that he (Freud) never conceptualized the cordial relationship which he established with the patient as a part of analytic technique although any part of the relationship remained open to later interpretation." (p. 236)

In fact, Freud (1913) elevated the idea to a principle that only after a "proper rapport" (p. 139) had been established (this manual includes rapport as part of the supportive component) could the therapist begin making effective responses to the patient's communications about the "hidden meanings of the ideas that occur to him" (the patient) (p. 139). (This manual refers to interpreting these hidden meanings as the expressive component of the treatment).

In trying to gain a good measure of trust and rapport therapists typically experience a natural temptation to impart to the patient information about themselves. The therapist may justify such behavior as necessary "in order to carry the patient along with them" or "one confidence deserves another" or "to put himself on an equal footing" (Freud 1912, p. 117). This temptation generally should be resisted since, on balance, it provides fewer benefits than it does potential long-term problems. It does not help patients toward becoming more aware of their own problems, and, in fact, it serves to distract them away from that focus. It may also make it harder for the patient to see the therapist as an impartial helper who can help work out the patient's problems.

Beginning to Understand and Respond to the Patient's Problems

Within the first few sessions the therapist already begins to form concepts of the obvious meanings and even the "hidden meanings" of the patient's relationship problems. These problems will often be related to the patient's symptoms and the goals that the patient sets up to relieve them.

In the first few sessions the therapist typically comes to understand much more about these relationship problems than is appropriate to take up early in the treatment, or perhaps ever. Some principles of selecting and timing responses will be mentioned here but elaborated later.

The first principle is that the therapist should have a rationale for selecting responses to the patient. The rationale should be based on a pre-treatment evaluation and on the patient's behavior in the early sessions. Its conclusions should be more specific than the patient's need for more or less supportiveness or expressiveness; it should contain "what needs to be supported and when and why, and what needs expression and why" (Schlesinger 1969, p. 268).

What needs expression typically is some facet of the central relationship problem. The therapist should then begin to focus his responses on aspects of the central problem. Maintaining such a focus is what is meant by a *focal treatment*, which is one of the hallmarks of the time-limited short-term psychoanalytically oriented treatments. The process of focusing on the main relationship theme continues throughout the treatment. Occasionally there is a major switch in that theme, but mostly there is a broadening and deepening of understanding of the theme. The details of focusing responses in terms of the core relationship theme are given in chapter 8.

After having decided what needs expression another principle needs to be relied on: the therapist should wait before responding until the patient is nearly aware of the problem. If this principle is disregarded, the therapist may "discredit oneself and the treatment in the patient's eyes"..."whether one's guess has been true or not" (Freud 1913, p. 140). This response principle applies to later stages of treatment as well.

6

Supportive
Relationships

A supportive relationship is necessary, according to the theory of psychoanalytic therapy, so that the patient will feel secure enough to venture to try to undo the restrictions in functioning that necessitated the treatment. The supportive relationship will allow the patient to tolerate the expressive techniques of the treatment (chapter 7) that are often the vehicle for achieving the goals.

Of course, all psychotherapies have supportive components, even the most expressive, because supportiveness is a usual and natural consequence of establishing a treatment relationship. Support can be, and typically is, derived from the inherent aspects of the treatment, such as the collaboration of the patient and therapist in trying to help the patient achieve the patient's goals. Freud (1913) recommends that the therapist should do nothing to interfere with the development of the natural inclination of the patient to become attached: "It remains the first aim of the treatment to attach (the patient) to it and to the person of the doctor. . . . If one exhibits a serious interest in him . . . and avoids making certain mistakes, he will of himself form such an attachment. . . . It is certainly possible to forfeit this first success if from the start one takes any standpoint other than that of sympathetic understanding" (pp. 139–140).

The sweeping beginning statement that "all psychotherapies have supportive components" has recently received quantitative support (Luborsky, Woody, McLellan, O'Brien, and Rosenzweig 1982). Three different treatments adapted for substance abuse patients were compared: supportive-expressive psychotherapy, cognitive-behavioral psychotherapy, and drug counseling. Two independent judges rated the degree of supportiveness expressed in segments drawn from these treatments. The three treatments were found to be virtually identical in supportiveness. This impressive finding occurs even though the SE manual is the only one of these three that accords a place to the role of supportiveness. Obviously a curative factor can exist whether or not it is accorded a place in a psychotherapy treatment manual.

What follows is a description of supportive techniques and their application. In reading this section it is necessary to remember a basic postulate of psychoanalytic theory (noted in chapter 2): A therapist cannot perform these techniques and assume that they are what they are. The attention of the therapist must be on the technique as it is experienced by the patient. Herbert Schlesinger stated this even more categorically (personal communication, 1983): "The patient has the right to define what it is that the therapist presents—it is a supportive technique if the patient experiences it as supportive." In keeping with this proviso, the rest of this chapter offers techniques that are generally considered to be experienced by the patient as supportive.

Deciding Which Patients Require Strengthening of the Supportive Relationship by Supportive Means

Patients differ in the amount and qualities of support they require. For many patients in SE psychotherapy the techniques can remain primarily expressive (chapter 7) throughout the treatment since its inherent supportive component is adequate. For such patients the expressive techniques can deal with the problems of experiencing adequate support and therefore the main techniques employed are similar to those of a well conducted classical psychoanalysis.

For some patients, the inherent level of supportiveness in the psychotherapy may need to be increased by extra special provision of supportive conditions. Those patients who are likely to require this are: patients with character disorders and disruptive alloplastic symptoms who have low anxiety tolerance and difficulties with being reflective, and patients for whom it is important to prevent regression and stabilize the level of adjustment by strengthening defenses and avoiding the analysis of defenses, since it may provoke undue anxiety and weaken defenses (Gill 1951).

Often the decision about whether and what kind of additional supportiveness is needed is clear to the therapist initially and remains so. For some patients, however, the decision about treatment techniques is difficult to make. The therapist may benefit from having the patient undergo a diagnostic psychological tests assessment (Rapaport, Gill, and Schafer 1968) or the therapist may gauge the patient's response through an initial trial period of treatment (Freud 1913), through trial interventions, or the therapist's decision may only come gradually and only after more experience with the patient's treatment, as was true for the two examples to follow. Ultimately, the therapist may even get some solace from knowing that such decisions about appropriate treatments for some patients have a special prayer proposed for them: "Lord, give me the patience to put up with things which I can't change, the strength to change things which I can change and wisdom to distinguish between the two" (this prayer has been attributed to various sources).

After a therapist comes to the view that a patient needs additional supportive techniques, providing them is usually experienced by the therapist as genuine and not as playing a role. Some therapists, however, are more comfortable with these techniques when they are not dignified by the term "techniques" but instead are considered as the helping behaviors of a decent human being (Lipton 1979).

When the decision is made to provide additional support it is necessary at the same time to decide what kind of support. Principles for making such decisions are offered by Schlesinger (1969). He concludes that the tendency to dichotomize treatments as supportive or expressive can be misleading:

> It would not be amiss on logical grounds to term that treatment "supportive" in which the psychotherapist must be ever mindful of the patient's need for support. But . . . when "supportive" is used as a typemodifier of psychotherapy, some therapists understand that the term requires the *exclusive* use of certain explicit supportive techniques and prohibits the use of certain other techniques (notably content and even defense interpretations). The term suppresses the therapist's interest and alertness to . . . whole classes of content of the patient's communications. . . . Supervisors of psychotherapy often hear a beginning psychotherapist report the painful gropings and musings of a patient who is struggling to master a painful conflict, and learn

that the therapist is aware of at least some of the underlying meanings of the patient's difficulties. When the therapist is asked why he did not help the patient by interpreting the situation to him he answers, in the full confidence that it is an adequate response, "The patient is schizophrenic," "The therapy is supportive." (pp. 271–272)

In Schlesinger's (1969) view, as in medicine generally, adequate diagnosis should lead to prescription of the forms of treatment. These forms are the varieties of supportive and expressive techniques used in SE psychotherapy. Diagnostic evaluations should lead to three sorts of specific treatment guidelines for applying the techniques: What in the patient needs support, how should the support be provided, and when is it likely to be most necessary. Patients often need support for self-esteem maintenance, for their sense of reality, for dealing with the over-severity of their conscience and for managing to modulate anxiety about their wishes. Examples of how and when support may be provided are offered below and later in this chapter.

EXAMPLE: Mr. Z.
A well known example of how hard it is sometimes to come to a conclusion on the issue of strengthening supportive conditions is provided by Kohut's (1977) reanalysis of his patient using altered techniques. The first analysis of this patient, which had a poor outcome, had relied on standard interpretative techniques (in this manual these fall into the category of expressive techniques). The second analysis provided an extra supportive component through the use of the therapist's empathy to bolster the patient's shaky self-esteem. Many of the therapist's interpretations took the form of recognition of how hard it must have been for the patient to tolerate his parents'

constant undermining of his self-esteem during his early development. Such responses have a strong supportive component along with an interpretative one and in the reanalysis they led to a successful outcome.

In the next example the therapist reevaluated the patient's progress after an initial period of treatment. She decided that a continuation of the ongoing techniques would allow the patient to become progressively even more upset and so unable to progress. Consequently she decided that more supportive components needed to be added and some expressive ones reduced.

EXAMPLE: Mr. P.

The patient was a 21-year-old white male college student. His view of why he came for treatment was unclear but he relied on the fact that "my father thought I should see someone." He had some concern that he had a generalized organic brain problem because of memory lapses, mostly for things he had done the day before. His girlfriend had recently told him that she was marrying someone else; however, it was only when he told his father about the loss that he realized that he was upset about it. The patient thought of himself as "cheerful" and "laid back" though sometimes he worried "am I shallow?" After the first session, the therapist recommended a neuropsychology evaluation. This showed that he had a superior I.Q. and there was no evidence of an organic brain problem.

The treatment was first discussed in the group supervision after ten weekly sessions. During those ten weeks, the patient had revealed that he had not told the therapist that he had not been going to class. He had taken incompletes and his advisor had gotten him a job as a resident advisor so that he could make up the incompletes. So far he had not started to work on the incompletes. He tended to come late for the sessions, and the sessions had many long silences.

In the last session, just before the patient was presented in the supervision group, the patient had told a dream: "I am in an area filled with women. They are attacking me. I shot back. I think this is a benign dream." The patient then revealed that he kept two pistols in his room illegally. The therapist now recognized more clearly the patient's obviously increasing feeling of being threatened by her. She began to think more about ways of quieting the patient's fear, by supporting his reality testing and independence of her, for example:

T: We could go over the dream, but it is more important that you do not accept things because I say them. You know better yourself about what you feel.

In the supervision session, the therapist expressed concern that her treatment technique could allow the patient to become more impulsive instead of continuing to be the "cheerful" and "laid back" person that he had been, and he seemed to be developing a suspiciousness toward the therapist. Toward the end of the review in the supervision session, it was decided that a more supportive approach was indicated since the patient had low anxiety tolerance and difficulties with being reflective. Techniques should therefore be used that would prevent regression and stabilize his level of adjustment. Instead of analyzing defenses, the strengthening of these defenses seemed in order. It seemed desirable not to interfere with the patient's defense of being "cheerful" and "laid back." The therapist had already started in that direction in her response (presented above) in which she took a position that would minimze the extent to which the patient perceived her as threatening.

It should stabilize his level of adjustment to function more adequately in his schooling. Therefore, the patient should be given the opportunity to review anything in the sessions that might interfere with his work on his incompletes. Furthermore, a new review of the patient's goals should be carried out. It would be important to know whether he agreed with his father's view that he "should see someone" or whether he had treatment goals of his own. It would be in order to review what has been accomplished so far, particularly the reassuring news that he need not be concerned about an organic brain problem. Finally, the patient was told how long the present therapist could continue the therapy before an expected change in jobs would occur.

In the next psychotherapy session, the therapist reviewed the patient's goals with him. She mentioned that since limited time was available, it would be good to know what he would like to work on.

T: What goals would you like to work on?
P: I don't know.
T: How have things been going with your school work?
P: I haven't done anything, so that is going to create a problem.
T: Would you like to work on that?
P: Yes, very much.

He launched on this by mentioning how overwhelmed he felt since he could not work on all the incompletes at once. P and T figured out that he could work on one at a time. The patient seemed much relieved.

Through this resetting of goals and through the other supportive measures, his morale and the quality of the helping alliance gradually improved. The therapist too felt relieved for she now felt she had understood better how the patient had been reacting to her before and had now instituted responses which were closer to those the patient needed.

Evaluating the Patient's Helping Alliance

The "helping alliance" (Luborsky 1976) is one term for a set of apparently similar phenomena reflecting the degree to which the patient experiences the relationship with the therapist as helpful or potentially helpful in achieving the patient's goals in psychotherapy. Two other terms which probably refer to the same phenomena are "therapeutic alliance" (Zetzel 1958) and "working alliance" (Greenson 1967)

High intercorrelations have been found among a set of patient's expressions in psychotherapy that were designated as evidences of the patient's experience of a helping alliance with the therapist (Luborsky 1976a; Morgan, Luborsky, Crits-Christoph, Curtis, and Soloman 1982; Luborsky, Crits-Christoph, Alexander, Margolis, and Cohen, 1983). These expressions of a helping alliance were moderately reliably rated by independent judges and significantly predicted the outcomes of psychotherapy.

Two alternative methods were developed, each with its own scoring manual (appendix 5), to measure the strength of the helping alliance: a global rating method(HA_R) for rating a whole session or segment of a session, and a counting signs method (HA_{CS}) for counting each specific example ("sign") in the session. The manual scores from each method were moderately highly correlated. Since both significantly predicted the outcomes of treatment, either one can be used when precise measures of the helping alliance are needed.

Both measures direct the judge's attention to the scoring of two broad categories of the patient's expressions: type 1, that the therapist is providing help to the patient and the patient is receiving it, and type 2, that the patient and therapist are working together in a team effort to help the patient. These

79

two types of helping alliance tend to be highly correlated, although type 1 is likely to occur earlier in the treatment than type 2.*

Both measures have very similar subtypes subsumed under the broad categories of type 1 and type 2. Since the subtypes of the two manuals are so similar it is sufficient to list here those in the HA_{CS} manual: it contains four subtypes of type 1: (1) the patient believes the therapist or therapy is helping, (2) the patient feels changed since the beginning of the treatment, (3) the patient feels understood by the therapist, (4) the patient feels optimism and confidence that the therapist and the treatment can help. Three type 2 subtypes are included: (1) the patient experiences working together with the therapist in a joint or team effort, (2) the patient shares with the therapist similar conceptions about the sources of the problems, (3) the patient demonstrates qualities that are similar to those of the therapist, especially those connected with ability to use the tools for understanding.

An unanticipated gain was provided by the HA_{CS} method in further understanding of the differential predictive value of positive vs. negative helping alliance signs. Early positive helping alliance signs were found to be significant harbingers of the eventual outcome of the treatment while the negative signs were much less reliable as predictors. This finding of the predictive value of the early positive helping alliance signs should

---

*Each method has different advantages. The HA_R has the advantage of greater simplicity since the session can be remembered or replayed from a tape recording and given a single set of global ratings on the subtypes. The HA_{CS} requires the time-draining effort of making a transcript and then searching it to find every example of the subtypes. The HA_{CS} method contributes to one kind of validity information about the probable bases for the global ratings derived from the HA_R. Even though the HA_R is called a measure of helping alliance, as is typical for a global rating method, it is not clear how the HA_R judge derives his ratings; the moderately high correlation of HA_R and HA_{CS} (e.g. 83 for positive HA_{CS} with HA_R) implies that the judge bases his ratings upon fairly literal expressions of the helping alliance of the kind described in the HA_{CS} manual (Luborsky et al, 1983; Alexander and Luborsky 1984).

give pause to those who are inclined to believe the clinical lore about early positive relationships as merely a "honeymoon" phenomenon. Rather, as in love relationships, it may be that "yes" (i.e., positive signs) means "yes" while "no" means "maybe." "No" here is equated with the negative helping alliance signs that have relatively little predictive value—some of these patients became positive later and improved, while some stayed negative and did not improve. Furthermore, this suggests a principle of technique. Negative helping alliance signs do not necessarily mean the treatment is destined for a poor outcome, but rather that the therapist should concentrate therapeutic work upon the negative evidences since they may be more involved in the patient's relationship problems. This technical principle appears to fit with Freud's principle of technique which, freely rendered, recommends riding along with the positive and interpreting the negative transference (Freud 1912a).

Facilitating the Patient's Experience of a Helping Alliance

Usually the patient's experience of a helping alliance will develop through the presence of a therapist who is doing the job of a therapist. The patient will recognize that the therapist is trying to help, the patient will then feel helped, and a good working alliance will form.

But sometimes the helping alliance needs strengthening and the therapist decides that it needs to be done by non-expressive means. In that case, which techniques can be used? A helpful set of therapist activities has been derived from the HA_{CS} subtypes by transforming each one into therapist activities that might foster it. The list of recommended therapist activities that follows was derived in this way and made a part of the therapist facilitating behaviors (TFB$_{CS}$ and TFB$_{R}$) manuals (appendix 5).

TYPE 1 METHODS*

1. Convey Through Words and Manner Support for the Patient's Wish to Achieve the Goals. The emphasis must always be on the patient as the source of the goals.

EXAMPLE:

T: When you started treatment you made your goal to reduce your anxiety. You see, in fact, we're working together to achieve that.

2. Convey a Sense of Understanding and Acceptance of the Patient. Freud (1913) recommends "sympathetic understanding" as a good attitude rather than moralizing or advocating a special point of view.

3. Develop a Liking for the Patient. The therapist's liking for the patient often helps in developing a helping alliance which in turn tends to be significantly associated with the outcome of the treatment. This association was found, for example, in Sloane et al. (1975). Since however, their rating of liking was made at the end of the four months of treatment, the therapists may have liked those patients who did well. But the converse is even more likely: that the liking for the patient had some impact on the improvement of the patient. In fact, in three of five studies where the prediction of outcome was made earlier in treatment, the positivity of liking was a significant predictor (Luborsky et al., in press).

*Type 1 means the therapist is experienced as providing help and the patient as receiving help.

Occasionally, the therapist may dislike the patient. On reflection, the therapist may realize that a countertransference issue is involved. No matter what the basis for the dislike, the therapist may find a corrective for it through trying the suggestion by Dr. Jan Frank (personal communication, 1951): "If you search, you can always find some aspect of the patient that you approve of and like. It is useful to make such a search and find that part." Another way to develop some liking, or at least sympathetic understanding, is to go through the process of formulating the patient's relationship problems. Through understanding the problems the patient must deal with, the therapist often gains a greater sense of acceptance and liking.

4. Help the Patient Maintain Vital Defenses and Activities Which Bolster the Level of Functioning. A useful way of providing supportive conditions is to evaluate the patient's strengths, especially the areas of competence and effective defenses and activities that have integrative benefits, and try to insure that the treatment will bolster them (Gill 1951). If, for examples, the patient is trying to get a job, hold a job, or complete his education, the therapist should be ready to explore with the patient anything that might interfere with these endeavors. This treatment recommendation is essential for patients who are severely ill, precariously in balance and might regress, and who can not use expressive techniques.

EXAMPLE:

T: I see you are helping yourself to feel better by finding ways to manage your job (or finding ways to get yourself through school).

5. Communicate a Realistically Hopeful Attitude That the Treatment Goals Are Likely To Be Achieved (or at least a willingness to continue to try to help to achieve them).

Being hopeful about the patient's future development in psychotherapy is not only a realistic attitude but can also be a beneficial attitude. Experienced therapists have observed its benefits, for example, Frank (1968), French and Wheeler (1963), and Menninger (1942, 1963). Many patients come to treatment at times when their problems seem overwhelming and when they are discouraged and depressed. The absence of hopefulness will make it harder for the patient, but the presence of hopefulness will make it more likely that the patient will continue to try and thus increase the chances of benefitting. Positive expectations and hope have generally been predictive of the outcomes of psychotherapy: in five of seven studies this was found to be true (Luborsky et al, in press).

EXAMPLE: Ms. N. M.
P: Everytime I try to take care of myself something bad happens. I explored some new ways of walking home from work and I got jumped and almost robbed and mugged so I get discouraged and helpless and I get into an attitude of not knowing where I'm going.
T: It's hard to feel you can keep trying since you've made a connection between keeping trying to take care of yourself and bad things happening to you.

The therapist conveyed in his response that the connection made by the patient was not a necessary one. Since it was a questionable connection, the patient could continue to keep trying. The attitude conveyed was essentially a hopeful one.

The maintenance of the patient's and therapist's hopefulness is realistic in the solid sense that it is supported by evidence from meta-analyses combining results of many studies. These studies verify the view that the majority of patients do achieve some of their goals in psychotherapy—they do "get better" (Bergin and Lambert, 1978; Luborsky, Singer and Luborsky 1975; Luborsky et al., in press, and Smith, Glass and Miller 1980). Happily, therefore, a hopeful attitude by the patient and therapist is justified. In the days when patients and therapists dressed more formally and consequently dressed more alike, this confirmatory story was current at the Menninger Foundation: A visitor to the Foundation, after telling a receptionist about her very positive experiences during her visit, queried, "but how do you tell the patients and the therapists apart? They all look alike." Receptionist: "The patients get better." This story faithfully reflects the fortunate fate of most patients in psychotherapy since it correctly conveys that patients in psychotherapy get better. Someone must have thought the story unfair to the therapists, for a sequel was heard: the same visitor visited a second day and came back and continued the discussion with the receptionist: "You must know a limited sample of the therapists. I talked to other receptionists and found that the majority of the therapists are also in psychotherapy, so they too get better."

Two other lines of research evidence back up the rationality of holding on to a hopeful attitude about the outcomes of psychotherapy for one's patients. Even though most patients can be expected to improve, the accuracy of prediction of the outcomes of psychotherapy for each individual patient is very modest (Luborsky, Mintz, Auerbach, Christoph, Bachrach, Todd, Johnson, Cohen, and O'Brien 1980). For example, it would have been very difficult for the therapist to make a prediction during the first year of minimal progress about the outcome of the treatment for Mrs. L. Fortunately, the therapist and patient did persist, for the patient made a dramatic, substantial resolution of the severe depression which had plagued her for many years. Similarly, it has been shown that the negative helping alliance statements on the patient's part early in treatment are not predictive of the outcome of the treatment while the positive ones tend to predict outcome.

It is sometimes difficult for the therapist to maintain a hopeful attitude when there is a long period when no progress is made. Several tried and true methods are available to support the therapist's task:

1. Remember that such periods are inevitable from time to time. Progress tends to be saltatory, not a smooth, gradual development.
2. Trust that after a while the therapist and patient will find what is causing the lack of progress. Then, when there is a turn toward increased progress, interest and optimism on both sides typically increases.
3. Review such long periods of no progress with a colleague. This step is useful even for highly experienced and competent clinicians.
4. When a stalemate continues, consider referring the patient to another therapist, or have the patient go through the process of making a new choice of therapist.

6. *Recognition, on Appropriate Occasions, That the Patient Has Made Some Progress Toward the Goals.* The helping alliance which typically develops as the treatment progresses can be fostered on appropriate occasions by recognition of signs of progress. The ultimate end-of-treatment goals are not attained in one powerful leap but rather by putting one foot ahead of another, with resting places along the way to get perspective on how far one has come. It helps considerably in sustaining motivation to arrive at milestones where one can look back to survey the distance traversed. Leonard Woolf was too extreme in the title of his autobiography, *The Journey, Not the Arrival Matters* (1969). The version of the title for the

psychotherapy journey should be modified to read, *The Journey's Many Milestones Matter, Not Just the Arrival.*

EXAMPLE:

> T: You noticed in what you just said, that you are feeling less depressed since you started treatment. You are making progress with your goal.

In the SE-TL version of psychotherapy particularly, it is good to have stored up some agreed upon achievements to point to against the day when termination arrives and full achievement of the goals may not coincide with the time of termination.

EXAMPLE (Ms. N., age 32):   Several times in the middle of the psychotherapy Ms. N. and the therapist shared the observation that even though the main goals had not yet been reached, it was clear that her work adjustment was markedly better. And even with the main goal there had been some improvement: she was still afraid and ready to turn away from men who were available, but she was less afraid.

7. Encouraging Some Patients to Express Themselves on Some Occasions. It can be useful for those areas in which the patient wishes to be helped. Sometimes the encouragement is best communicated by noting the non-expression and the topics on which it occurs.

TYPE 2 METHODS*

1. Encourage a "We Bond." When the therapist experiences a helping alliance with the patient, it will tend to get conveyed and will facilitate the alliance. The therapist will

---

*Type 2 refers to the patient's experience of working together in a team effort.

reveal his or her experience of the existence of the bond in many direct and indirect ways, such as in the use of "we" illustrated in many of the examples in this chapter.

2. *Convey Respect For the Patient.* This is the opposite of behavior that could cause the patient to feel put down (for example, by humor at the patient's expense).

3. *Convey Recognition of the Patient's Growing Ability To Do What the Therapist Does in Using the Basic Tools of the Treatment.* The therapist shows an acceptance of the fact that the patient develops an ability parallel to that of the therapist in terms of valid self-observations.

EXAMPLE:

T: Yes, you now see how we work. You and I are both using the same approach and working along the same lines. (This is also an example of a "We bond")

EXAMPLE: The following is an example of the therapist's sensitivity to the patient's wish to say in his own way what he understood: The therapist had just given several responses containing his understanding of what the patient had just presented. Each time the patient gave a nodding but perfunctory agreement.

T: I noticed you nodded in agreement each time I said what I understood. I believe you agree, but you may have your own way of understanding what you just expressed and would like to say it as you understand it.

4. *Refer to Experiences That the Patient and Therapist Have Been Through Together.* In that way, the patient and therapist build up a familiar joint backlog of common experiences.

EXAMPLE:

T: You and I have become familiar with that kind of problem. It's the same problem we talked about with [an-
other event both of them have become familiar with].

5. *Engage in a Joint Search for Understanding.* It may seem
jarring at first to see the joint search for understanding included under supportive techniques. After all, the SE Manual's
techniques are organized around the dichotomy of supportiveness vs. expressiveness, with understanding presented under
expressive techniques (in the next chapter). Actually, the
search for understanding can often be accomplished in a way
that not only does not upset the patient but also provides
support. Searching for, and from time to time coming up with,
understanding can have tremendous supportive value for the
patient. Aside from the direct utility of the understanding, the
fact of achieving it can be viewed by patient and therapist as
an evidence of progress in the joint therapeutic endeavor.

7

Expressive Techniques: Listening and Understanding

The techniques in this chapter are called *expressive* because through them the therapist sets the stage for the patient to express thoughts and feelings and to listen and to reflect on them, with the aim of understanding and changing what needs to be changed. Much has been written about these techniques, for they are supposed to be the mainstay of psychoanalytically-oriented psychotherapy. Some of the usual directions for the use of these techniques (Wallerstein, Robbins, Sargent, and Luborsky 1956) are that the patient should be provided with as much of an expressive component as he can handle. This component will be greater for those patients with adequate ego strength and anxiety tolerance, along with the capacity for reflection about their interpersonal relationships.

Acquiring Understanding: The Four Phases

For much of the time that the therapist is engaged with the patient in a session, attention should be primarily upon the basic task: to listen to what the patient is communicating (listening); to evaluate it (understanding); and then to decide how to communicate that understanding (responding). The therapist experiences the process of understanding as an alternation of these three plus one more phase: Listening, Understanding, Responding, and Returning to Listening (table 7.1 summarizes the essence of each phase).

TABLE 7.1
The Four Phases of the Expressive Task

Phase 1 *Listening:* Listen at times with an open receptiveness to what the patient is saying. If you are not sure of what is happening and what your next response should be, listen more and it will come to you.

Phase 2 *Understanding:* Understanding will happen from time to time, but patience is necessary. The understanding will come in the form of understanding the patient's intentions and their consequences, especially as they affect the main area of suffering expressed in terms of the main symptoms and the theme of the central relationships, including the relationship with the therapist.

Phase 3 *Responding:* Tell the patient some of what you understand of (1) and (2) (above) in ways that will reach the patient. Do not worry as much about how you tell it as about being sure that you get your message across.

Phase 1' *Returning to Listening:* Free your mind to return to listening with an open attitude but also keep in mind listening for the patient's reaction to your previous response.

PHASE 1: LISTENING

The forms of listening are varied. They correspond to three types of occasions which require a listening phase:

1. This occasion occurs most often at the beginning of sessions when the therapist is content to listen freshly and to set aside for the moment any hypotheses he has had in mind before. During this form of listening, attention is relatively open and unreflective. Freud (1912b) described this form of attention as "evenly suspended." In prescribing the therapist's attitude during such listening Freud (1912b, p. 112) says, "He should simply listen and not bother about whether he is keeping anything in mind." Although, inevitably, the therapist has some preconceptions—often useful ones—based on all of the information and hypotheses he has about the patient, these should be kept tentative to allow for the possibility of new impressions being considered.

The fact that the treatment method is called psychoanalytically oriented psychotherapy does not mean that the therapist should look for any particular dynamics; instead the method advocates an empirical attitude, an openness to hearing what the patient is presenting. Otherwise the therapist's conceptual model could be a hindrance to listening. Only after such listening, the therapist may sometimes remember that what the patient presented fits a particular theory, but should not try to make it fit.

2. A form of listening occurs when the therapist needs to arrive at good hypotheses to help in dealing with a pressing issue in the treatment. These are times when the therapist feels an urgency to form such hypotheses in order to be able to respond to the patient. Often, with this attitude, the hypotheses will appear.

However, some therapists may feel impelled to respond before they understand the patient's meaning and consequently their response may be off the mark. Freud (1912b, p. 112) adds some reassurance to the therapist: "It must not be forgotten that the things one hears are for the most part things whose meaning is only recognized later on." It is a natural part of the treatment process that there will be periods in which the therapist does not yet understand the patient's message. The therapist can handle the consequent discomfort by means of the reminder that if the understanding has not yet come, it will come with further listening.

3. Another form of listening occurs on those occasions when the therapist wants to check the accuracy of his or her hypotheses. On these occasions, the therapist listens to hear how the patients's statements bear on the hypothesis. Such listening serves to enable the therapist to affirm, discard, or revise the hypothesis.

In essence, listening, in all of these forms is an integral part of psychoanalytically oriented therapies. As contrasted with other types of psychotherapy, the therapist in SE psychotherapy must listen in order to know how to respond, since he or she does not come prepared with a preset message. The structural position of listening in psychoanalytically oriented psychotherapy is aptly revealed in the Talmud by the question of a young rabbi and the answer of his senior rabbi. Young rabbi: "Why is it that we have two ears and only one mouth?" Senior rabbi: "Because it was meant that we should listen twice as much as we should speak."*

PHASE 2: UNDERSTANDING

The forms of listening just described in phase 1 are essential preliminaries to phase 2, which is the achieving of understanding. In phase 2, the therapist relies on a more reflective, evaluative, understanding attitude as hunches and hypotheses de-

*With thanks to Dr. Merton M. Gill for alerting me to this source.

velop. The gain from a shift in mode of listening has been shown experimentally (Spence and Lugo 1972). Both the therapist and patient eventually understand more and more about two facets of the patient's communications: (1) the most interfering symptoms and psychic pain and (2) their interpersonal context. This context is composed of both inner and outer conditions precipitating and continuing the symptoms and psychic pain. The inner conditions are versions of core conflictual relationships; the outer ones are the behaviors of others that appear to the patient to fit into the core conflictual relationship template.

Especially in supportive-expressive time-limited psychotherapy (SE-TL) and other short-term focal psychotherapies, it is necessary to make an accurate decision within the first few sessions about the main relationship theme or some aspect of it, for it should become the focus of the therapeutic effort. Coming to an understanding about the main relationship theme has been viewed as an intuitive process (e.g., Mann 1973), but there are some clear principles to help guide this intuition:

Principle 1. Understanding the Symptoms in the Context of Relationships.

The appearance of symptoms or evidence of pain and shifts in these in the course of a session should be a focus of the therapist's and patient's attention. The obvious rationale for this focus is that the patient comes for psychotherapy to get help for symptoms and for other problems that restrict or cause pain. The first listening task of the therapist and patient should be, therefore, to locate these symptoms and attendant suffering and to understand how they come about.

Since the word "symptom" was used as one of the nodal events around which the attention of the therapist should be focused, it is necessary to define it. "Symptom" is defined here in a broad sense (as in Freud 1926) as a dysfunction of a usually intact function or capacity. For example, a momentary forgetting is a dysfunction of memory in the sense that we usually can remember the thoughts that we have just intended to say. Such symptoms and their related affects, most often anxiety and depression, as well as shifts in these, tend to appear in most sessions.

Both clinical experience and clinical-quantitative research with the "symptom-context" method support this recommendation to focus understanding around symptoms and related affects. That method has been applied to recurrent symptoms which appear during psychotherapy sessions, such as momentary forgetting (Luborsky 1967, 1970; Luborsky, Sackeim, and Christoph 1979), cluster headaches and stomach pains (Luborsky and Auerbach 1969); petit mal attacks (Luborsky, Docherty, Todd, Knapp, Mirsky, and Gottschalk 1975), and precipitous depressions (Luborsky, Singer, Hartke, Crits-Christoph, and Cohen 1984). Two examples follow, each from a different patient.

EXAMPLE: Ms. N.

The therapist recognized by his comment a repeated association between the patient's showing a strong affect of sadness with having her attractiveness noticed. In this session and many others, it was established that the sadness appeared because she was reminded at such times of her never having gotten such recognition from her father whom she both loved and resented. The resentment came from her tremendous fear that she would be forever closed off from that kind of appreciation and intimacy with a man because having a man would mean what it meant to her mother: having to endure hiding her strength and knowledge to please the man. Her mother, in contrast to her father, was consistently warm and supportive to her. These relationship problems were central in maintaining her main symptom: an inability to tolerate a relationship with a suitable man as a long-term partner.

T: Each time I notice and comment that you are looking attractive or that you're doing well in your work you get tearful and cry.

P: (crying) I feel I'm not attractive. I feel I will be rejected. Father could never stand it. I won a ribbon in a race and he only could say the competition was not too great. Dad did the same restricting with Mother. She even had to limit her vocabulary for him.

T: I see, so you feel you have some well established old reasons for feeling that way with me.

EXAMPLE: Mrs. L.

For the first 10 minutes she spoke with enthusiasm about her involvement in many different activities, such as being involved in a research study. Her mood began to shift and she became less excited. Her speech began to slow:

T: What's happening?

P: I began to be depressed when I sensed you were losing interest and I was, therefore, isolated and could do nothing about it.

T: At first you had felt I *was* interested.

P: Yes, but then you began to lose interest. That's what people tend to do. Like when I told the class about the research of a woman who treated diabetes. Now a man has come along as though he were the first to make a contribution and has shown the same effect with animals.

T: So you caught your whole sequence beginning with a good feeling and then noting that when you saw me as being less interested, you began to feel depressed and alone.

P: Yes, I began to feel like a cloud was on my brain. I think of it physically. I've discovered that the way to pull out of it is to become active—and that does work.

She began to talk, to tell avidly again about the history of the cure of diabetes.

In the above example, the therapist commented on the patient's shift from spontaneity and enthusiasm to boredom and depression—which was one of the main initial symptoms. The shift gradually became understood in terms of the central relationship problem. She had become afraid of showing the spontaneity to the therapist. She was also afraid of showing it to her boyfriend, and earlier she had been afraid of showing it to her parents. It was the central frustration she experienced during her growing up. She felt that what she wanted was unimportant as compared with pleasing them by being quiet and not expressing what she wanted. If she persisted, she felt she would hurt them, especially her father, whom she saw as fragile and depressed, and then she (the patient) would become guilty.

Principle 2. Attending to Shifts in the "States of Mind".
Small shifts in the patient's condition within sessions may reflect shifts in larger constellations. These larger ones are worthy of being called *states of mind,* as they are termed in a system of "configurational analysis" by Horowitz (1979) or as "intra-individual trait factors" (Luborsky 1953). It is worth identifying these larger shifts for they give broader meaning to the many smaller shifts which compose them. Moreover, the

contexts for these larger shifts in state often reveal the triggers for the shift, as in this example:

EXAMPLE: Mrs. L.

When the patient reported a small shift into what she called "cloudiness," it was part of a larger state including not only cloudiness but greater depression, poorer memory functioning, lack of competitiveness, low mood, and greater distance from the therapist. The therapist also noted at the time of the shift the concomitant cloudiness beginning with the patient's having stopped pressing her view that the therapist's curtains should be changed. This led the therapist to the inference that the meaning of having stopped pressing her view of what she wanted was instrumental in the shift in state. When the therapist interpreted that, as noted in the example earlier, the patient's mood became better.

Principle 3a. Formulating the Core Conflictual Relationship Theme (CCRT) by Clinical Methods.

Psychoanalytically oriented psychotherapists recurrently need to formulate and reformulate the main transference relationship theme and within that, to locate the main relationship problems. Such formulations are an especially pressing need in focal psychotherapies where an aspect of the relationship theme is selected as the focus of the therapeutic work. The guidelines for discerning these relationship themes are unusually explicit in this manual. They were developed in response to the frequent question of clinicians, even experienced ones: "How do the most expert clinicians do this and how well do they agree?" Because of the importance of this principle, three examples are presented below. The first two are examples of fairly typical clinical formulations of the main relationship problems related to the main symptoms (Mrs. M. and Mr. Q.).

The third is an example of a clinical formulation aided by the CCRT method (Mr. B. N.).

EXAMPLE: Mrs. M.

This patient's main symptoms were anxiety and absence of sexual feeling. She experienced the anxiety as being based on her absence of sexual feeling. This example is presented because it is one where anxiety was recurrently reported and could be identified in the relationship contexts in which it occurred. A few of these condensed contexts excerpted from a selection of sessions are given below. In reviewing them, attend to the hypotheses that will occur to you about the context in which the anxiety occurs:

P: When I was growing up, about the ages of 15 to 18, I was going with a boy whom my parents, especially mother, objected to. I thought there was nothing wrong with him. I don't know why mother objected to him. She never said. I kept on going with him. He is the first one I went on to a sexual relationship with. Mother and I had arguments and I said I have a right to go with whom I wish. She crumbled. "I could never do that to *my* mother," she said. I was UPSET and I had some guilt over that. I don't know whether I should have guilt.

P: We [husband and the patient] did make love after playing around. During the playing around I felt okay, but then in making love I felt I couldn't, I couldn't say, I couldn't tap him on the shoulder and say, "Stop." I get very ANXIOUS and uncomfortable.

P: I remember now suddenly my first boyfriend. That was around age 13. We really liked each other. I used to think about touching him but I wouldn't. The relationship was just playful, so it was okay. But I wouldn't even hold hands. I wanted to very much, but I couldn't. He'd say, "You have to," which made me ANXIOUS.

P: I had a good weekend. Spent a lot of time with [husband]. Ever since last week when he said, "You know, we could spend a lot of time with each other without having to have sex," it's been easier. We had no sex. I felt better that that was okay, and was NOT UPSET anymore.

P: I'm feeling better now about myself (gets ANXIOUS and tearful) but he [husband] is deprived.

The relationship theme which is most evident in these episodes can be formulated as a wish and the consequences of the wishes. The wish is: "I want to feel free and spontaneous," for example, "playing around"; the consequences are: If "I go ahead, especially with sex, I lose control to the other person since it becomes a must to go ahead. It then upsets and depresses me if I do, and I don't enjoy it. So I decide. I will avoid any such wishes or activities where I might lose the feeling of being free, spontaneous, and retaining control. But when I keep control, then the other person is hurt and that upsets me."

In this theme, therefore, anxiety comes at two junctures: (1) if she loses spontaneity or a sense of control and the other person is seen as having it, with her having to comply, or (2) if she retains control in the face of what the other person wants, she sees the other person as "crumbling" or "deprived" and not having control.

EXAMPLE: Mr. Q.

Relationship themes are pervasive in psychotherapy sessions. They are especially clear within the immediate context of a symptom's appearance, as we have seen under principle 1. Three brief consecutive examples are presented here for Mr. Q., a 23 year old veterinary student whose main complaint was depression. The beauty of having a sequence of examples from a single patient, each centered around a shift in depressive mood, is the heightened clarity with which the relationship theme emerges when the clinician attends to the redundancy in the examples. After each example some inferences will be drawn about the relationship theme; at the end, a clinical formulation of the main relationship conflict is given based on all three examples together.

EXAMPLE: 1a

In this excerpt, after talking about his girl friend and telling a dream he had had about her the night before, the patient said, "That just made me a little tight, I don't know why (voice drops)."

(The expression *a little tight* means that the patient was anxious; *voice drops* suggests, as the transcript goes on to confirm, that the patient was becoming depressed. In the rest of the excerpt it is clear that the therapist was attending to the shift in the symptom or, more exactly, to slight changes in affect, for he inquired of the patient what had started to make him "tight." The patient reported the depressing thought: ". . . a guy like me could be with her but, you know, . . . I'm not strong enough." The patient was competitively comparing himself with another "guy" and coming off short. That theme, which might be part of the patient's relationship problems, is manifest in what the patient was talking about just before the shift into depression occurred.

The larger segment of example 1a follows containing the shift in mood along with 100 patient word segments before and 100 patient word segments after the shift:

P: . . . I can see that there's a g—a great deal of truth in that and that uh you know me—I mean you know she'll either have to marry someone who's (i.e., weak)—or spend her life with someone who's unbelievably strong and self-confident and, you know, like sh- or someone exactly like her so that they never really do have any encounters aside from very active and superficial ones and they never do get to know each other. Or else someone [100 words] like me but a million times more than me. I mean someone who is kind and good to her but just tr-tr-*tremendously* strong. And not- By strong I mean self-self-confident. But she- she- so I mean- but I dreamt about her. You know it wasn't- it wasn't any special kind [50 words] of dream, I mean, it was just uh you know, I mean it was- I don't remember what it was but it wasn't anything remarkable and there was no sex involved in it and there was no- I don't know, we were just talking or something or something like that. **SHIFT POINT** *So that-that just made me a little tight I don't know why.* (voice drops) **END SHIFT POINT**

T: What made you tight? Just now?

P: Talking about her. Yeah.

T: Can you catch what was starting to make you tight?

P: No I don't remember.

T: Was it what you said or what you thought?

P: Just the thought of her I guess. Oh I know what it was, you know, I've got it.

T: Uh-huh.

P: It was that I said well a guy like me could be with her but you know a million times stronger. Eh you know as [50 **words**], if it's me then I'm not strong enough. That's what bothered me.

T: Yes.

P: You know. Sort of. I-I mean so I mean I know y-you know that that's what she is and th-that's it you know unless some unfor-uh tragedy happens to her th-you know for some reason she weakens then [100 **words**] then but you know again see I- that's why I feel bad cause it's means I-she's stronger than me, or brighter than me. I mean she is brighter than me, I guess, but hmph y- well this that's what's bothering me, see. I'm comparing again. She's rough. Okay . . .

EXAMPLE *1b*

P: . . . this girl that works in the library, the divorcée. I mean we're just going to lunch. We're going out. And, uh, you know, that-that's bad cause, I mean, you know, she's a sexually experienced woman and, uh, you know, I imagine she enjoys it, you know, and what am I gonna do, you know, what, what if she loves me. I mean, cause I think she does. I mean, you know, she thinks- she thinks I'm nice, y-you know. So I don't know (pause) sort of a problem (yawn). But (exhale) (pause). **SMALL SHIFT POINT** Now what, huh? I don't know what to do or (voice fades)

T: At that moment it feels like there's not gonna be anything else that'll come through your mind that, that you —

P: Well it sort of—

T: —were gonna say—

P: —makes me feel bad.

T: What does?

P: When I don't have anything to say, nothing now. I don't know why. You know this guy B.? (voice brightens)—on depression? . . . (low voice) (long pause). So now what? I don't-I don't have anything to say. (clears throat) (pause)

T: There must be some thought there about your not having anything to say that makes you feel bad.

P: Well it does make you feel—
T: There must be some thought there that explains your feeling bad now, here with me.
P: I can't figure out what it is. If-if it's just, uh, well I can talk about it we'll say and if it's that I-can't-talk sort of thing, I-I have nothing to say therefore I'm bad, you know, I don't—
T: Yeah
P: —I don't think so though. 'Cause it's sort of it's a feeling of helplessness, of uh futility that well I won't get anything here either sort of, you know, cause well we're not doing anything but sitting, sitting on my ass 'n you know, sitting 'n that- that's all I can expect out of anything 'n that's why, 'n that's why, that's where the bad feeling comes from, I guess (yawn) (very low) you know, that's all.
T: Yeah.
P: I don't know what else.

In the last example the patient stops near a small shift in affect and says, "I don't know what to do," and begins to get depressed. The therapist inquires and finds that the patient is blaming himself because he has nothing to say. The patient is angry at himself for not performing. He is not talking, feels inadequate because he is not talking, and then gets depressed because it means to him that he is inadequate. He is probably also feeling inadequate to deal with the "divorcée." The patient is close to the idea also of talking about a related problem in the relationship with the therapist. The patient tried to bridge the distance with the therapist by asking whether the therapist knew a man he knew, "this guy B." The problem is that the patient feels he will not get any recognition from the therapist. The patient has decided that the therapist did not pass his relationship test, for he says, "we're not doing anything but sitting." The therapist should then have explored more explicitly the patient's feelings about the relationship. Not only is the patient feeling inadequate but it is also likely that he is feeling the therapist is not doing anything to make him feel more adequate, and, therefore, the patient decides the therapist, too, is inadequate.

EXAMPLE *1C*

This example shows the same sequence of listening, followed by understanding the context of the shift in the symptom:

P: Well, I don't know. I probably just felt bad about it. I didn't want to fight with him (i.e., father).

T: That's exactly what you did. You felt that you had to feel bad everytime you thought of sticking him on his ass.

P: Yeah, but I never did.

T: You never did but you often wanted to.

P: Heh, no, I don't-think I ever did wa- think of-. Y'k-now, I don't-I mean- there was never anything to fight about. Well there was thing—reasons to fight—okay, I guess I am s-. I hate 'im now sometimes but (sigh), I mean, he never did a damn thing. He was useless. He made money. I mean, all right, I will consider him within the- his historical milieu and, and, blah-blah-blah and Depressions and not having anything to eat and all that shit- But I-I-I don't know. **SHIFT POINT** This- this just confuses me. This isn't doing me too much good.

T: Why not?

P: I don't know, 'cause I don't feel good now again.

T: Well what was- what did you say that made you not feel good right then?

P: 'Cause I just got all back and depressed again when I wasn't, I was out 10 percent then.

T: That's right, you were. Then catch what made you feel all depressed again.

P: Something about my father, I guess.

T: Yes.

P: I don't know. I was fighting him or something.

T: Yes.

P: That I hated him.

T: Yes. Yes.

P: Why I had to feel guilty about—

T: Yes.

P: —hating him?

T: Yes.

P: Well, I guess you do. You have to love your father, and all that shit.

T: Right. Yeah. And so if you hate him and you feel like fighting him and setting him on his ass, then you have to feel depressed about the whole damn thing.

P: And it's therefore I feel that way with all males.

T: Including this male talking with you.

P: Yes.

The patient was depressed in this session but had gradually begun to come out of it until the painful point in this example marked *shift point* when the patient got depressed again. The therapist noted the shift in symptom and then attended to the context for this shift. What was revealed was that before the shift the patient had been angry at his father because his father could not be admired for what he was and did. Apparently just before the shift the patient began to feel guilty about his anger with his father.

As just demonstrated, the relationship theme emerges with increased clarity after additional examples are inspected, as we can see through reviewing the three examples. They all concern the patient comparing himself with another person, usually a man. Then he usually feels inadequate or decides that the other person is inadequate. In example 1a, the shift in depressive mood came after the thought "I'm not strong enough" to compete with the guy for the girl. In example 1b, the shift came when he was comparing himself with a woman who was more sexually experienced than he was and he could not defend himself against feeling inadequate. Then he became silent and began to feel inadequate in relation to the therapist because of the silence which implied to the patient that he had nothing to say. In example 1c, the shift came when he wanted to put his father down because of the father's inadequacy. Then he blamed himself for his hostility to the father and got depressed. The essence of the main relationship theme can be stated in the form used in the core theme formulation. In these three examples for Mr. Q., and in other examples from the same patient, the relationship theme as expressed in paraphrased form in the first person is: *Wish:* "I want to feel I am adequate in comparison with another person, usually a man." *Consequences:* "I feel painfully convinced of being inadequate. Sometimes I become self-blaming for wanting to put down someone else like father and then I become depressed." In essence, this formulation combines the main symptom with the main relationship context in which it occurs.

Principle 3b. Formulating the Relationship Theme by the CCRT Method.
The focus of the clinician's attention in formulating the relationship themes is not restricted only to understanding the context of symptoms and their associated pain; it is often based

on finding the pattern of the patient's relationships with others. A version of this approach will be illustrated by the CCRT method applied to a psychotherapy session (see the example in appendix 4 and for more detail, Luborsky 1977; and Levine and Luborsky 1981).

This method is unique in its power to expose the principles of clinical judgment underlying formulation of a relationship theme, since it provides a more objective and quantitative system for doing what the clinician does ordinarily. For the researcher it is the first relatively rigorous method for deriving relationship theme formulations from psychotherapy as well as determining the amount of agreement achieved by different clinicians.

Several somewhat similar methods are being developed. Configurational analysis (Horowitz 1979) is a system which incorporates the CCRT and describes changes in psychotherapy. Another near relative of the CCRT method is a coding scheme for evaluating the patient's experience of the relationship with the therapist (Gill and Hoffman 1982a). The scoring scheme catches both direct and indirect references to the relationship; this division roughly corresponds to whether the connections are made explicit by the patient or the analyst or whether they are inferred by the judge. Yet another system is an even nearer relative. It is used to formulate the patient's "unconscious plan," based upon clincal evaluation of the first sessions of psychotherapy by a group of clinicians (Weiss and Sampson 1984). Some research studies have been confined to estimating the amount of transference (Luborsky, Graff, Pulver, and Curtis 1973) rather than, as in the CCRT method, on identifying the type of relationship theme.

The CCRT method is based on three main refinements of the clinical method for formulating the central relationship theme:

1. The unit for inspection and scoring can be limited to the "relationship episodes" within sessions instead of the complete sessions. Relationship episodes are the narratives about their interactions with other people that patients tell in the course of their sessions. Use of such episodes simplifies the task of identifying the CCRT.

2. The CCRT is expressed in a standard form as a sentence containing two main components (figure 7.1): a statement of the patient's wish, need, or intentions; for example, "I wish something from (a person)" and a statement of the consequences of trying to get one's wish from that person; for example, "but I get upset" (a consequence from the self) or "but I will be rejected" (a consequence from the "person"). The

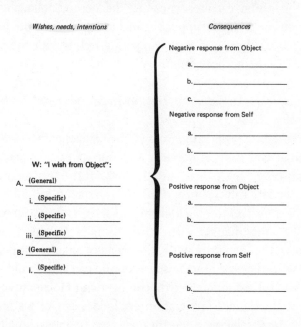

Figure 7.1 *Format for the Core Conflictual Relationship Theme Formulation. (Types of components are listed in order with the most frequent first).*

CCRT can be thought of in Freud's terms as the patient's perception of certain types of danger situations evoked in relation to people (Freud [1926]1959). These danger situations typically involve expected or remembered helplessness and, therefore, are often associated with anxiety.

3. The task of the clinical judge in doing the formulation is markedly simplified by finding the components that are most prevalent. After reading and rereading the relationship episodes, the clinical judge will be able to pick out the theme which is expressed most frequently throughout the relationship episodes.

An example of the application of the method to the patient, Mr. B. N., is presented in appendix 4. After reading samples from the session, each reader can try the method, following the directions given in the appendix, including filling in the blank CCRT Scoresheet and then comparing results with the filled out CCRT Scoresheet Summary.

Principle 4. Attending in Turn to Each Sphere of the Relationship Triad.

To achieve a rounded picture of the main theme, it is valuable to attend to its appearance in three spheres: (1) current relationship of the patient and therapist in the treatment; (2) current relationships outside of the treatment, with family, friends, co-workers, et al.; and (3) past relationships, especially with the parent figures. Two of the examples presented earlier illustrate the application of this triad-of-spheres principle. They show the way a therapist's attention can and should shift from one sphere to another (Menninger and Holzman 1973). It helps the patient arrive at an expanded view of his or her relationship problems when they are seen to appear in all the spheres. The patient can then more readily acknowledge the problem and see it as "my problem."

EXAMPLE: Ms. N.

The therapist first related a behavior which occurred outside of the treatment; for example, "You're trying to do well in your work," to behavior which occurred inside the treatment; for example, "You get tearful and cry when I refer to your attractiveness." Then the patient further understood her getting upset after she spontaneously turned her attention to the third sphere, that is, her relationship with her father: "Father could never stand my being attractive." The content of these three spheres is a reflection of the main relationship theme: *Wish:* "I wish I could find a suitable man to provide me with the physical and emotional support I need," *Consequence* (response from self and from others): "but I shouldn't because I am independent and I can't because I will be rejected and the man will not be able to provide that kind of support."

EXAMPLE: Mr. L.

Again in this example a shifting of attention to each sphere in turn occurs. The patient was speaking with enthusiasm about his current activities outside of the treatment; for example, "I am enjoying taking pictures for the Yearbook." The therapist says when he observes a shift, "What's happening now?" which calls attention to the current shift in mood within the treatment session; a turning away from enthusiasm and toward depression. Eventually the third sphere, his past relationships with his parents, is brought into the focus of attention; for example, "my parents would not listen to me." Again, as in the earlier example, each of the spheres partially reflects the main relationship theme: *Wish:* "I want to be able to achieve and be recognized for it"; *Consequence:* "but I shouldn't be and will not be, especially because it might hurt my brother or father."

It is not necessary routinely to bring into focus all three

spheres in the same session, although doing this from time to time is useful. What we have called earlier the "redundancy of the theme" in the three spheres is the overlap; its content helps in deciding what is encompassed by the CCRT. The diagram in figure 7.2, the above two examples, and especially the three examples for Mr. Q., all illustrate this method.

Of the three spheres, attention to the current relationship of the patient and therapist has the greatest potential for therapeutic impact because their interaction is played out in the "here and now" (Gill 1979). The therapist should attend closely to the patient–therapist relationship because the fluctuations in that relationship provide the central arena for the activation and then the potential resolution of the patient's relationship problems. In fact, it is a good guide for the therapist to remember that if the patient is unusually upset, and particularly if the onset

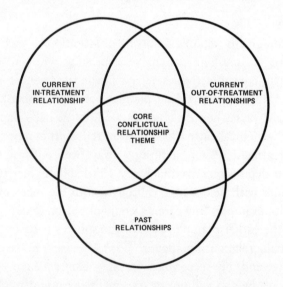

Figure 7.2 *The Triad of Relationship Spheres with the Core Conflictual Relationship Theme at their Intersection.*

of the distress relates to one of the sessions, its cause might be found in the current relationship, both in its transferred and real components. Taken together, the current relationship with the therapist, the current outside-of-treatment relationships, and the related early relationships are likely to be a reflection of the transference pattern or, as alternatively labeled here, the experienced actualization in the current relationship of the CCRT (as shown in the last few examples).

In addition to listening for the triad of relationship spheres, Holzman (1965) points out the value of concurrently using another set of frames. The therapist should listen for the continuities in the themes of three time samples: (1) between different aspects of the present session; (2) between aspects of the present session and the one immediately prior to it; and (3) between the first two and the longer series of sessions.

Principle 5. Further Reviewing Tends to Produce Further Understanding.

It is a well-known observation among clinicians that further review either with or without a supervisor produces further understanding. Reviewing can be done before, during, or after the sessions. As a practical device, consistent with Holzman's (1965) point, just before the patient is seen it is often helpful to refresh one's memory by reviewing the most recent session or series of sessions. The review can be done either with or without the aid of brief process notes which contain a few memorable parts of the sessions plus the essence of the session (as described in chapter 4).

The essence of the session represents a more abstract level of meaning and is a good way to store the larger view of the process. Such staying in touch with what has happened between patient and therapist in the immediate past can be valuable for the conduct of the psychotherapy. It can, of course, be done even without consistent recourse to reviewed notes. As therapists have often noticed, even when at the beginning of a session the therapist did not recall where the patient had left off, once the patient was launched the recall would recur reliably.

The value of such retrospective views, reviews, and overviews was the point of Rudolph Ekstein's tale (personal communication 1951) about a type of crow that was always seen flying backwards. On one occasion some neighboring birds asked these crows to explain their strange behavior. They crowed in reply, "We're just more interested in seeing where we've been than where we're going. And besides," one crow added as an afterthought, "we really get ahead better by knowing where we've just been."

At the same time, having an agenda of some intentions based on the review of earlier sessions can *sometimes* be a hindrance. These intentions may have to be restrained so that they do not intrude on a properly fresh attitude toward listening to the session that is about to convene. If the new session is a proper forum for proceeding with the intentions, there is no problem about carrying out the agenda. If it is not, one had better stay with what is developing.

Principle 6. Seeing the Symptoms as Problem-Solution or Coping Attempts.

The symptoms can be understood as faulty and costly attempts at problem–solution, usually of relationship problems. Seeing the symptoms as problem–solution attempts and using language with the patient reflecting this view is useful to both therapist and patient. One of the virtues of formulating the CCRT in terms of wish and consequence sequences is that it leads the patient and therapist to think in terms of faulty problem solutions. After discerning the wish–consequence theme and thinking of the consequence as a trial solution, listening further will then allow one to hear other alternative solutions. It is usually best for the patient to come up with these alternative solutions, and if they are not labeled clearly by the patient that way, the therapist should do it. Theoretically, there are always many possible solutions; practically, it may be difficult to tell which type of solution is the one the patient can and will try.

EXAMPLE: Mr. G. E.

The initial main symptoms were overeating, overweight, and compulsive masturbation. His core relationship theme was, *Wish:* "I want care"; *Consequence:* "I know I won't be given it, so why try." Moreover, he felt, "so why try to get over the symptoms. They are more reliable supports than direct attempts to get what I want." After the theme was reviewed with the patient, his subsequent thoughts contained several attempted solutions. The first was to force himself to stop the symptoms by an act of will. The patient rejected this one, saying that he was not able to do it that way. In fact, he resented doing it that way. The second was to stop wanting anything from anybody. The patient decided that he had tried from time to time and did not like it. The third solution was to start trying again to stop the symptoms with the attitude that he could combine doing his share of self-control with getting directly what he needed from others. That solution seemed to him to be a workable one.

Principle 7. Attending to the Patient's Perception of the Therapist's Behavior.

All of the patient's responses to the therapist can hardly be based on erroneous perceptions resulting from seeing the therapist through the distorting lens of the patient's CCRT. The therapist's characteristics and behavior are often seen clearly, although the patient might interpret them in terms of his or her CCRT. The relative contribution of the patient and therapist to the patient's perception varies from occasion to occasion, extending from those that are highly patient stimulated to those that are highly therapist stimulated. It can be valuable therapeutically for the therapist to recognize his or her stimulus value on each occasion. (This principle, therefore, also constitutes a response principle and belongs in the "response principles" section.)

EXAMPLE: Ms. X.

(This is really a therapist's in-house joke serving to illustrate a point.)

A woman patient phoned her therapist very early one morning. She was very upset and said she had to see him immediately, even though she knew it was earlier than their usual appointment time. He gave her an early appointment in which this exchange took place:

P: I had this very upsetting dream, so I had to see you immediately. I grabbed a Coke, put on my coat, and here I am. The dream was this: A figure appeared to me in the dream. It was very scary. I looked at the face. It was the face of my mother. Then, I looked at the back of it, and the face on the back of it was your face. I have to know the meaning of that dream!

T: (pause) You had a *Coke* for breakfast! Do you call that a breakfast!

This example, of course, is apocryphal. It exemplifies a highly therapist-stimulated patient response. We are not told whether the therapist was able to recognize his stimulus value. Presumably, he was unable to do so.

116

This next example illustrates the helpfulness of distinguishing the patient's *perception* of the therapist's behavior from the patient's *interpretation* of that behavior, usually in terms of the patient's readiness to see things in terms of the CCRT. The usefulness of identifying and recognizing the therapist's role in the patient's response is emphasized by Gill and Hoffman (1982). They describe a coding method whose focus is on "an important first step in the analysis of transference: the identification and exploration of the preconscious points of attachment of transference ideas in the here-and-now. Related to the scheme is the view that there is a generally plausible basis in the here-and-now for the patient's ideas about the therapist" (p. 166).

EXAMPLE: Mrs. L.

Mrs. L. wanted the therapist to change the curtains in his room. The curtains "depressed" her by their "lack of change." The patient had mentioned in earlier sessions that she wished the therapist would change them, but they did not change. The patient saw this "nonresponsiveness" by the therapist, as a sign that the therapist was not interested in paying attention to her wishes. Furthermore, she also interpreted the therapist's behavior as based on disapproval of the patient's assertiveness and competitiveness. After saying all this, the patient lapsed back into a cloudy state, not knowing why she was in treatment and what she wanted out of it. Thereafter in the session, the therapist recognized the obvious fact that the curtains had remained the same, but that the patient had interpreted the sameness as reflecting the same kind of discouragement of initiative and assertiveness that she had experienced from her parents. The patient's mood became better and she became more active and involved.

Principles of Inference Making

Now that specific principles for understanding patients' main communications have been discussed, it is of interest and value to stand back and abstract the basic principles which operate to assist the clinician in making inferences. The three most reliable, and those most used in the examples presented are:

PRINCIPLE 1. ATTENDING TO REDUNDANCY

This is the most used and most useful principle. When more than one instance, for example a symptom context, is available from the same patient, the principle of redundancy across contexts can contribute to understanding. Inspecting the contexts in sequence allows recognition of significant redundancies in the components of relationship themes. In the first example of a mood shift context of Mr. Q., the patient is talking with a man about competition for a woman in which he feels tremendously inadequate. In the next example of a mood shift the patient is also feeling inadequate in relation to his father and also devaluing his father. In applying the redundancy principle across examples, in both of these examples the theme involves comparison with or conflict with another man in which the patient feels inadequate and self-blaming.

PRINCIPLE 2. ATTENDING TO TEMPORAL CONTIGUITY

This is a commonly used principle for deriving understanding in many of the examples. It means that if two thoughts follow each other, they may have some causal connection. Also, the more often they follow each other, the more likely a causal connection exists. Temporal contiguity may be between successive thoughts or within or between each of the sequential components in the typical symptom–context sequence: (1) pre-symptom, (2) symptom, (3) postsymptom.

PRINCIPLE 3. ATTENDING TO SHIFTS IN STATE

The workings of a psychological system tend to be more fully exposed to view during its shifts than during its stasis. This third principle is utilized in the examples of shifts of depressive mood (Luborsky et al. 1984) and in the method by Horowitz, Marmar, and Wilner (1979) and Horowitz (1979) for analyzing shifts in state during psychotherapy. Lastly, it is evident in a new field, "catastrophe theory" (Berlinski 1978), for aiding in exploring drastic state changes in psychological as well as physical systems.

8

Expressive Techniques: Responding and Listening Again

Responding

After listening (phase 1) and achieving some understanding (phase 2), the therapist becomes better prepared to respond (phase 3) in terms of expressive aims. To guide this phase the therapist can follow certain principles, including listening again after a response (phase 1'). Listening which is followed by understanding, typically yields much more than would be appropriate for any one response by the therapist. There are three questions to be considered by the therapist when selecting and fashioning a response: what to say, how to say it, and when to say it. The first 7 of the 13 principles listed below deal with the first element. They are the most essential ones and they are all related to principle 1. Of these numbers 1, 2, and 3 are to be relied on most and are therefore preceded by an asterisk.

PRINCIPLES OF RESPONDING

Principle 1. The Therapist's Response Should Deal Effectively With a Facet of the Main Relationship Problem and At Times Relate That to One of the Symptoms.

This first principle takes up the first question: What should the therapist say? In essence the principle suggests that:

(a) Each response should be about one strand of the main relationship pattern or the essence of the pattern. While engaged in each session, the process of listening and understanding, as experienced by the therapist, is like tracking a "red thread" across a field (to use Dr. Ellen Berman's analogy). The thread comes into view only from time to time. When it reappears it may be greeted with the surprise associated with the rediscovery of the familiar or with the satisfaction of a broadening of one's understanding. The red thread corresponds to the clinical formulation of the main problem. A more objective version of the relationship problem can be provided by the core conflictual relationship theme method (CCRT); the CCRT therefore constitutes an objective method of achieving a focus for the therapist's responses.

(b) The strand chosen for each response should be one that is close to awareness (Principle 8) and not too heavily defended against in the current session (Bibring 1954; Glover 1955).

(c) Some of these responses should also be related to the main symptom or main pain, especially any that appear in the current session.

EXAMPLE:

This example is from the sequence of three examples of Mr. Q., presented earlier under Understanding (chapter 7):

The therapist's response each time a shift in mood occurred was first to call attention to the fact that a shift had just taken place. What the patient said thereafter gave the patient and therapist an opportunity to listen for the ideas associated with the shift in mood. (a) In the first example the patient's thoughts were about being inadequate as compared with another man in his ability to get the woman he wanted. For this patient, it is clearly a facet of the patient's main relationship theme which is relatively accessible to the patient's awareness at this point. (b) In the second example the initial response of the therapist was again to make a comment pointing to the fact that the patient had just gone through a change in mood. At this point the patient began to think about it and realized that the conflictual relationship issue is, "I have nothing to say, and therefore I'm bad", that is, inadequate. The therapist responded by asking for the thought which connected having nothing to say with the self-blame, "I'm bad." (c) In the third example again the therapist pointed out a shift in mood; again the patient explored the thoughts associated with the shift in mood. The therapist responded by asking further about the connection and the patient came to realize that he was talking about being angry at his father for his father's inadequacy and then felt bad for being angry. That thought sequence had led to the return of his symptom of depression.

This series of three incidents also illustrates that after the main relationship theme was formulated, and the therapist responded by noting the change in the patient's symptom in the session, the larger frame of associated themes began to emerge. One of these is shown in the second example: When he is speaking of his own inadequacies, he attributes them to his not speaking. Then he comes to the thought, "We're both not doing anything," implying that the therapist is also inadequate. This idea appears even more clearly in the third example where again, but more directly, the other is seen as inadequate, in this case his father. The new strand then, which adds to our understanding of his sense of inadequacy, is that his own inadequacy is attributed both to his father's and the therapist's inadequacy. These people are thought to be responsible for not getting him what he needs so that he could feel more adequate.

With the supportive–expressive (SE) therapeutic system which utilizes attending to the appearance of symptoms and related pain, how should the therapist deal with a session in which these are not evident? One answer is that the response principle is not essentially different. The therapist can deal with the content of the session by relating it to previously reported symptoms and pain; another is that there is no need always to relate the relationship problems to the symptom.

EXAMPLE: Mr. H.

The patient spoke about the extreme work load under which he was working but now, in contrast to what had always been true before, he did not find it a source of anxiety; he was handling the load quite well. Most of what he said in the session referred to the kinds of problems which he had presented in previous sessions when he was not handling the load well.

In this session, the therapist and patient followed the course of noting the improvement and contrasting it with the kinds of relationships with parents and wife which formerly had charged the context for handling work pressures in ways that had vastly increased the sense of external pressure.

Principle 2. The Therapist Should Recurrently Recognize the Core Relationship Theme Since It Facilitates the Working Through.

After hearing principle 1 of Responding, a therapist in training asked, "What is left to say to the patient after the core conflictual relationship theme is once interpreted?" A therapist came to Freud ([1914]1958) with the same question; Freud replied by explaining the necessity for working through the central relationship problems in the transference. The working through is identified by Freud ([1914] 1958) in "Remembering, Repeating and Working through" as a process which facilitates the patient's change in the course of therapy by offering opportunities to reexperience the relationship problems as they appear in the three spheres, and particularly in the one with the therapist, that is, in the transference.

This reexperiencing and working through provides a variety of gains to the patient; they constitute what is learned in psychotherapy:

a. An increase in ability to identify the cues to recognition of the central relationship problems. These cues for identification are necessary since the relationship problems typically reappear in many seemingly different contexts.

b. An increase in ability to distinguish what the patient brings to relationship problems vs. what other people and other events bring to them.

c. A greater recognition of the power of the core relationship problem. As one patient put it, a crucial part of mastering the core relationship problem is "to recognize its slippery power to reappear."

d. An improvement in recognition of how the core relationship problem relates to other relationship problems.

e. An increase in insight into how the relationship problems might have originated. In the example on Mr. Q. in chapter 7, the relationship problem may have gotten started because of the patient's view of the father's inadequacy and the patient's identification with his father.

f. A greater understanding of how the relationship problems serve a function that perpetuates the problems so
that the person derives a "secondary gain" from them.
After having reexperienced the relationship problems
many times it becomes natural to explore in what ways
their continuance serves a purpose.

g. A greater range of problem solutions is acquired for
dealing with the relationship problems. It should not be
a surprise that even after long periods of working
through, the relationship problems remain recognizable,
since they tend to be deeply embedded in the patient's
behavior. Fortunately, in addition, the patient generally
acquires increased mastery of them, especially in terms
of altered consequences to the wishes, such as lessening
of self-injurious behavior.

EXAMPLE: Mrs. M.

Mrs. M.'s core relationship theme was: "I want to be free
in relationships but if I get involved, especially sexually involved, I lose control." For that patient, as her treatment
continued, the theme remained prominent but it became better delineated. Further meanings of it gradually appeared, including its functions, one of which was to keep the patient tied
to her mother who was mainly responsible for initiating the
sexual and related relationship problems. In the course of the
treatment she worked out some ways of combining being involved sexually with preserving a greater feeling of control.

*Principle 3. The Therapist Should Recognize the Patient's
Need to Test the Relationship in Transference Terms.*
Not only does a revival of the transferred relationship prob-
lems occur in the relationship with the therapist but the revival

also serves the patient's need to test the relationship with the therapist. Weiss (1971), Sampson (1976), and Silbershatz (1977) find that patients follow an "unconscious plan" which plays a part in the patient's decisions on ways of proceeding in treatment and even on when the patient can safely bring out issues in the relationship to test the therapist's response. During and after these tests the therapist can play a helpful role by remaining neutral, by not behaving in ways which are expected of the patient's traumatizing early "objects," and by helping the patient to recognize that these are transference tests.

EXAMPLE: Mr. Q.

In these excerpts from two sessions the therapist responds by pointing out that the patient is testing the relationship with the therapist. It happens also that the test is in terms of the general relationship theme which is at the heart of the transference problem.

P: I heard the details of the good job you did in handling the staff problem in your department. I must tell you.

T: You want to see whether in our relationship you, and I as well, can tolerate your saying to me that I am adequate.

(Next session)

P: I thought over what I heard about the job you did with the staff problem in your department. I don't see it was much of a contribution. It really was just common sense.

T: You want to see whether you, and I as well, can tolerate your wish to put me down and to try to make me feel inadequate.

Principle 4. The Therapist Should Recongize That Both Therapist and Patient Find It Especially Hard to Deal With the Patient's Experience of the Relationship With the Therapist.

Of the three spheres of the core conflictual relationship theme (CCRT) method, the hardest one for both the patient and therapist to deal with openly is the relationship with the therapist; consequently it is the one most often skirted. Freud (1912a) considers one obvious basis for this on the patient's part: "For it is evident that it becomes particularly hard to admit to any proscribed wishful impulse that has to be revealed in front of the very person to whom the impulse relates" (p. 104).

This neglect is especially unfortunate since the patient–therapist relationship is potentially the most profitable arena because it is where the "tests" of the relationship are carried out and need to be observed. When the tests are passed and understood, special power is conferred upon the patient through his or her having "confronted the lion" by learning about the central relationship problems by direct and immediate observation in the here and now. Much of this arena's power for inducing learning is conveyed by the presence of both patient and therapist as participants and witnesses of the unfolding of the patient's relationships in thought, feeling, and action.

When psychotherapy sessions are reviewed by the therapist or reviewed in supervision, the evidence becomes obvious that there is special difficulty in responding therapeutically in this sphere. It is not that the supervisor or others who are engaged in the review have a higher therapeutic intelligence than the therapist (although one of Morris Parloff's famous quips appears to apply: "the role of consultant confers an automatic advantage of 25 I.Q. points over the consultee"), but rather that the "consultants" gain the advantage of a reviewer's position in the freedom to be a Monday morning quarterback and conduct their review in an atmosphere less encumbered by the emotional enmeshment of the patient and therapist with each other.

Some more precise forms of evidence testify to the relatively greater difficulty of responding in this sphere as compared with the other spheres: (a) The match of messages test (chapter 8) and the rating scales for the therapist's responses show this (appendix 5). For example, it is shown in the ratings on such scales as "the degree to which the therapist's response passes the patient's test of the relationship with the therapist", or "the degree to which the therapist's response is directed to the most emotion-laden or pressing part of the patient's transference issue in the session." (b) The research of Gill and Hoffman (1982a) provides a way of estimating the quality of the therapist's response to the patient's experience of the relationship. (c) The Weiss and Sampson (1984) research focuses around the degree to which the therapist passes the patient's tests.

Two kinds of therapist problems in dealing with this sphere were identified on the basis of discussions with therapists during supervision, after presentation of the account of the sessions: (a) the therapist had not been aware during the session of the evidences of the transference, or (b) the therapist was aware of the evidences but neglected to deal with them. A frequently effective correction for the first is for the therapist to have more practice in CCRT formulation and, during the sessions, to try varying his or her attention to permit some mental review periods as a preliminary to possible responses.

Typical explanations by the therapist for the second type of problem are, "I didn't know at the time how to respond to them," or "I was afraid it would upset the patient so I didn't bring it up." Further discussion with the therapist provides greater understanding of the therapist's dilemma and reasons for not responding. In making a bridge to the patient's awareness it helps to have material from what the patient says or does which is close to the patient's awareness of its relevance to the relationship with the therapist. Often the discussion with the therapist in the supervision will suggest types of responses to the therapist that he or she can now use. At times, role-playing of possible responses can help the therapist solve this problem.

However, sometimes the therapist appears to be justified in holding back since the contemplated responses might have hurt the treatment relationship. The therapist might correctly estimate that the patient's experience of the relationship is not close enough to awareness for the therapist to be able to present a response that the patient could understand.

EXAMPLE: Mr. D.

Throughout the session, the patient spoke about several women, all of whom trampled on and overlooked his needs, and he felt caught and unable to take care of his needs. For example:

P: I was trying to enjoy the day off of work and do what I wanted to do, but mother called me to deliver some papers to her downtown, to park the car and come looking for her at the place where she works. I can't say no. I want to say no.

T: You feel caught.

P: Yes, even with (girl friend). She forgot something and wanted me to go all the way back to the house to get her lunchbox, and I should go. I just wanted the day for *me*. At work, I now choose to have a schedule but I run around listening to everybody but myself. The pressure is mounting.

T: It sounds like nobody listens to your needs.

In the discussion, after the presentation of the session, the supervisor and the group members all noted that the therapist had responded in terms of the outside-of-treatment relationships but not about the relationship with the therapist, and that this had been true for the entire treatment. The therapist and the others who reviewed the session all agreed that the explicit experience of the relationship with the therapist was positive but the implicit one was filled with the obvious material that the therapist had not so far responded to. The therapist said she was afraid it would alter the positive relationship she had with the patient which had been so helpful in his considerable progress. The supervisor agreed that this was important with the patient but that it would be helpful to begin the process of allowing the patient to talk about the nature of his relationship with the therapist; for example, to say: "With the women that you mentioned, your mother, girl friend and others, you feel your needs aren't taken into account and you have to go along with their wishes. Generally, here with me in this relationship, you feel free of that although you may feel that at times." Such a comment would be a first step in suggesting to the patient that the relationship with the therapist is something that he can talk about.

EXAMPLE: Ms. G.

In the first months of the treatment the patient recurrently described her situation while she was growing up; it seemed to her to be somehow involved in her adult relationships. She was made to do much of the hard housework in the rooming house her mother ran. At the same time her mother did not show her any signs of love or of recognition for her work. The men in the rooming house did show her love but that made her angry, depressed, and guilty. The relationship with the therapist was mostly parallel with the one with her mother and sometimes with the one with the men. The therapist never referred to these parallels, even though there were many signs in the treatment of the patient feeling starved for affection and recognition from him and of her trying to say it directly but being unable to. The therapist explained in the supervision that he was afraid to discuss it with her directly because if he did it would make it even more obvious that he could not give her what she wished and it would have the effect of making her even more frustrated and depressed. Once the therapist expressed this explanation in the supervision it became more possible for him to quiet his fear by understanding that the patient could realize her partly transferred relationship problems and instead could feel more recognized, accepted, and supported if he were able to make explicit the sources of her frustration with him.

Principle 5. The Therapist Should Stay With the Main Relationship Theme Because It Provides a Focus Which Furthers the Alliance and Sense of Progress.
After the main relationship theme is first presented and with each new appearance in which it is recognized, it becomes clearer and clearer to both therapist and patient. The therapist may then say to the patient at an appropriate time, "We begin to see the problem in your relationships which you are trying to solve. The issue is—————." Such a formulation provides a renewed focus; it also increases the sense of progress by the "we now see" and the sense of alliance conveyed by the use of the word *we.*

EXAMPLE: Mr. H.
The patient is aged 30, and his outstanding symptom is depression. This example illustrates the principle of staying with the theme. Early in treatment, the therapist summed up as follows:

T: I see. You are mostly bored and discouraged in your work and you're unable to develop the relationships with friends that you wish. So you feel really stuck in your life.

The patient responded very affirmatively for he felt understood; he then began to explore his state of being stuck. After further listening to what the patient was saying, the therapist was able to add:

T: I remember you told me that your father was the one who was always involved in doing interesting things and you were there on the sidelines, bored and discouraged, holding the flashlight for him while he did the interesting work.

After a few sessions of similar exchanges around the meaning of the discomfort and pain of being stuck, a clearer and clearer view of the patient's main relationship theme gradually emerged and with it came more of a sense of progress and alliance. The wish, which was now more clearly stated was to get unstuck by deriving enjoyment from his work and a sense of pride from it. His typical "consequences" were that he felt on the sidelines and became bored and depressed and it was only when he realized that he was depressed that he inferred that what he had been doing was on the wrong road. He then began to try other newer "consequences," such as ways of realizing enjoyment in his work and ways of enjoying taking time off from work.

Principle 6. Achieving the Goals of Treatment Requires a Different Degree of Working Through and Attendant Insight for Each Patient.

For some patients just a brief period of working through and related insight into relationship problems is sufficient. For other patients much more of this work is required to achieve the necessary change. Similarly, for some patients small changes in certain areas of functioning can make a huge difference in general functioning (Brenman 1952). Based on analysis of retest results, Schafer (1958) came to a similar conclusion.

The example given for Ms. N. (p. 75) was one where a huge amount of effort by the patient and therapist in working through the meaning of the object choices in terms of the wish formulation was necessary before the patient became able to tolerate the choice of a suitable man. Long before that was achieved, another central goal having to do with competence in her work was much more easily attained. A good rule of thumb for the therapist about how much effort to put into the working through is to go as far as is needed to achieve the goals, so long as the patient's motivation is maintained.

Principle 7. A Matching of Patient's and Therapist's Messages Serves as a Test of the Therapist's Response in a Session.

One test of the adequacy of the therapist's response that has stood up well in practical applications might be called the matching-of-messages test. It works in this way: in reviewing a session, either during or after it, the therapist can consider what is the main message of the patient, what is the main message of the therapist's responses to the patient's message, and how adequately did the therapist's responses address the patient's message? The formulation of the patient's message can be done in the usual clinical manner by reviewing the session in one's mind with an occasional assist by process notes (such formulations are likely to be similar to the more systematically achieved ones guided by the CCRT). The formulation of the message in the therapist's responses is arrived at by the same kind of review. A good session is one in which there is a reasonable match between the two messages.

Some research experiences with the matching-of-messages test are available. The concept was first applied in one study under the label "therapist responds effectively to the patient's main communication" (Auerbach and Luborsky 1968). A rating scale for this is provided in appendix 5. Three judges, working independently, were able to rate this variable with moderately good agreement (.65, $p. < .01$). In that study the procedure followed by each judge was first to specify the patient's main communications, then to specify the therapist's responses to them, and then finally to see the extent to which the therapist dealt with the patient's main communication in a reasonable and effective way.

EXAMPLE: Mr. B. N. (see appendix 4 for transcript)

To estimate the appropriateness of the therapist's responses in this session the reader can proceed intuitively as if he or she were the therapist engaged in the session, or the session can be reviewed after it has been read. The reader also may wish to try the more precise CCRT way by formulating the patient's message as measured by the CCRT. For the patient in this example, the CCRT was derived independently by four research judges. The CCRT represents the components with the highest frequencies. The wish component is: "I want to assert myself by maintaining my strength, my opinions, and my competence." The consequences are: (a) response from the self: "I go along or I withdraw," (b) response from others: "I am dominated or I am rejected."

This CCRT can be taken as the patient's "message." To estimate the adequacy of the therapist's responses to it the patient's and the therapist's messages need to be compared. The simplest way to do this is by reading over the therapist's statements which are numbered in the transcript in the appendix. The therapist's first responses (as numbered in the margin), for example T1 to T7, are mainly supportive. The therapist opens with T1, "How have you been?" or T6, "We were talking quite a bit about that last time." The more expressive side of the session starts with T8 in which the therapist explores what the patient is wishing for in relationships. In T14, the therapist is pointing to the patient's need to assert himself in relationships, and then in T17, the therapist explores the same issue of first feeling "more alive" in the relationship with the therapist but then getting frightened and wanting to withdraw. Rather than continuing to explore that issue, the therapist feels it necessary to reassure the patient about the patient's withdrawal, as shown by the patient's silences.

As a whole then, the therapist's responses show a moderate approximation to the patient's message. However, the therapist does not make his responses clearly enough in terms of the patient's relationship problem with him in this session (maybe because it is only the third session).

Principle 8. Responses Should Be Timed to Take into Account How Near the Patient Is to Being Aware of the Content of the Proposed Response.

This is a standard principle in all accounts of technique of psychoanalytically oriented psychotherapies. Decisions about proper timing are not usually difficult to make. They depend on the therapist knowing how much the patient knows and how much has been gone over with the patient before. Usually the consequences of poor timing are not serious unless one is egregiously off the mark. The therapist mainly needs to relisten and get recentered or refocused as in principle 1 of Responding. It is therefore usually poor timing if at the beginning of treatment the therapist responds with inferences about certain deep wishes, as Freud, noted (1913, p. 140), for example, "but what a measure of self-complacency and thoughtlessness must be possessed by anyone who can, on the shortest aquaintence, inform a stranger . . . that he is attached to his mother by incestuous ties."

Principle 9. The Extensiveness and Complexity of Each Interpretative Statement Should Be Limited.

It will facilitate the patient's learning if the therapist does not make statements in each response which are too long or too complex. When too much is presented at once, it may be hard for the patient to take it all in, for it may diffuse the patient's attention rather than focus it on the main point. Furthermore, it is better for the therapist to give responses piece by piece and be guided by the patient's response to each piece.

EXAMPLE: Mrs. L. (see p. 96).

Note in the example that the therapist's responses are presented piecemeal.

Principle 10. The Therapist Needs Patience and Restraint About Responding Interpretatively Until the Therapist's Understanding Is Adequate.

The best reassurance for the therapist is the reminder that it is natural not to understand consistently. By its nature, understanding comes saltatorily, not gradually and evenly. There is no point, then, in responding to the patient just for the sake of responding, or to avoid a silence, or even to be drawn into implying to the patient that understanding exists before that is really the case. The therapist can keep anxiety about the performance as a psychotherapist in check by accepting the idea that the necessary understanding and knowledge about how to respond will come in time. If it is not there at the moment, it will come in a while. Further listening and reviewing will produce further understanding (as in principle 5 of Understanding, chapter 7). That acceptance is a precondition of patience, and is very good for patients and therapists alike.

After working together for a while, a parallel process will develop in patients, who will also become more tolerant of delays in understanding their communications. It is a common observation that when patients get discouraged by not understanding what they are saying and ask to have it explained, that within a short time after asking such a question, further listening by patient and therapist will reveal some of the answers (even with no direct interpretation from the therapist).

Principle 11. Responses Should Be Timed to Take Into Account the Length of the Session.

It is often good to listen for the first 5 to 10 minutes before responding, in order to get a sense of the main issues the patient is beginning to present. Then, most of the therapist's responding should be done in the next 30 minutes. The last 5 to 10 minutes of the session is not ordinarily a good period in which to introduce new topics, since not enough time may be available for the patient and therapist to deal with them.

Principle 12. Countering Countertransference.

It is easy to get caught up in certain kinds of counter-therapeutic responses to the patient. However, when they appear, the therapist can deal with them better if their varieties are known and distinguishable (Singer and Luborsky 1977). Four of the main types are described below:

a. The classical countertransference response is the counterpart on the therapist's side of the patient's transference reactions. In this case, it is the therapist who is responding to the patient in terms of the therapist's relationship problems with his or her own "archaic objects." As indicated already, the best way to protect against this type is to have had sufficient experience with it in the past, usually through the therapist's personal psychotherapy, so that it is recognizable after a while and, therefore, more amenable to correction.

b. Responsiveness without sufficient reflection and understanding usually occurs as a result of becoming overinvolved in the exchange with the patient, so that it is difficult to do the necessary occasional distancing involved in reflecting on and reviewing the exchange.

c. A *contagion* of mood is the term suggested by Redl (1966) to help explain interpersonal transmission of affects; for example, if the patient is depressed, the therapist becomes depressed, if the patient is happy, the therapist becomes happy, and so on. When the patient is most caught up in involvement in relationship problems, he or she is likely to be experiencing the most stress. The stress will probably be a shared stress since the therapist also tends to feel it, but in attenuated form. This mutuality of emotional response was illustrated by the simultaneous psychophysiological recordings of patient and therapist by Greenblatt (1959).

Alertness to the existence of this phenomenon in psychotherapy helps to preserve the therapist's equanimity and helps to avoid persistent sharing in the patient's mood (Butler and Rice 1963). Extremely field-dependent therapists may be more apt to get caught up by such contagion, as suggested by the work of Witkin, Lewis, and Weil (1968), and Witkin (personal communication 1970). On balance, however, moderately field-dependent therapists might be more helpfully responsive to the patient and form a better helping alliance (Luborsky, Crits-Christoph, Alexander, Margolis, and Cohen 1983). Moreover, highly field-independent therapists might be likely to stay so uninvolved and overreflective that they will appear cold and unable to form a warm relationship with the patient.

d. This type of response occurs when the therapist behaves in ways that fit into the patient's negative expectations and fears. Such negative fitting into the patient's negative expectation is more common than has been supposed, as Singer and Luborsky (1977) have shown. For example, if the patient is communicating a fear that people dominate him or her, the therapist may unwittingly begin to do just that. Apparently the patient does something to stimulate this reaction from the therapist, but it is not known how this is accomplished. The therapist is more protected from falling into such counter-therapeutic responses if a reasonable balance is maintained between listening with some involvement versus listening with some uninvolvement. When, through this way of listening, the therapist has become aware of the main theme of the patient's relationship problems, this awareness serves as a further protection against fitting into the patient's negative expectations.

EXAMPLE: Ms. K. U.

The patient was a woman graduate student, age 28, whose main problem was fear of breaking away from her parents and developing in her work and starting to go out with men. The patient expected that her parents would not support her in growing up and in separating from them. They appeared to her to do things to keep her tied to them. They were critical, for example, of her manner of presenting herself in job interviews.

The supervisor and members of the supervision group noted that the therapist somehow did not notice the patient's moving ahead with her work in graduate school and the increase in her thinking about her social life. The therapist responded to this observation by reflecting that he now realized that he seemed to have gotten sucked into fitting her negative expectation that he wouldn't notice evidences of her growth.

Principle 13. "Near responding," The Inclination to Think of Responding Countertherapeutically, Provides a Good Basis For Understanding the Patient.

This inclination to respond countertherapeutically often is thought of by the therapist as an interference. Instead, recognizing these inclinations toward responding has a positive value for understanding the patient. This principle is discussed here since it follows directly from the section on countertransference and its understanding tends to lead directly to useful responses.

EXAMPLE: Mr. J. P.

The therapist reported to his supervisor that in the last two sessions with the patient he had felt bored, inclined to reject the patient, and ready to respond with irritation. He felt he could do nothing but sit and listen to the patient's tremendously repetitive accounts. Each time the therapist had tried to respond therapeutically, the patient felt criticized. The therapist therefore felt trapped and required to sit and listen to the patient while enduring the frustration of the lack of progress.

After reviewing this impasse with the supervisor, the therapist and supervisor came to the formulation that the patient was engaging in a test of his relationship with the therapist. The terms of the test were that the patient was seeing whether the therapist would accept him. However, acceptance to the patient meant that the therapist would not do anything that smacked of being in the role of a therapist. This was reviewed with the patient with considerable benefit to both participants.

Phase 1': Returning to Listening

After responding, the therapist returns again to listening but this renewed listening is a new listening phase. It is new in the sense that now the therapist knows the patient's response to the therapist's response. Knowing the patient's response helps in guiding the therapist's next response. In choosing each succeeding response to the patient, the therapist not only should select from the formulation of the CCRT but also take into account the patient's response to the previous response. The patient's response usually provides bases for more understanding of other branches of the CCRT. It is not necessary, therefore, for the therapist to place all his or her bets on each response because clues will come from the patient's responses about which way to go—whether to go on in the same direction or alter course.

It is hard for the therapist to keep the balance between openness to what the patient is saying at the moment and recalling past themes of the patient's relationship problems. It takes energy to shift back and forth, and it takes energy to keep the openness in the face of the recall of what was evident before, to take in new information and, if necessary, to revise hypotheses.

Fortunately, ability to keep the balance between openness to new evidence and recall of themes is a skill which can be developed. The skill is based partly on the knowledge of the principles of listening, understanding, and responding as described in this manual. The therapist's knowledge of these principles has the effect of lowering the therapist's anxiety and, therefore easing the job of listening, understanding and responding (Spence and Lugo 1972).

9

Ending Treatment

The patient usually begins to consider termination seriously because the goals of the treatment are becoming achieved. At that point staying in treatment becomes less necessary. Nevertheless, when termination is considered, how the patient and therapist behave in response to its approach is largely what would be expected of two people who have become important to each other and are about to separate. This chapter is organized around five basic ways in which the patient and therapist deal with the anticipation of the separation. For each of these, the manual includes recommendations for the therapist, (listed below), primarily aimed at minimizing the stress of the separation and insuring that the gains of the treatment have the best chance of surviving:

1. The patient and therapist remind each other of when the termination will take place, so that they will be prepared. It is recommended that the therapist reclarify the time structure at this point.
2. The patient and therapist talk about the conditions under which termination will come about. It is recommended that the therapist recognize preliminary cues

about the patient's conditions for termination; mark treatment phases so they serve as milestones; recognize the "arrival" in terms of the achievement of goals; recognize that the achievement does not mean that all problems are gone.

3. The patient and therapist may lose hope of ever achieving goals and arriving at termination. In this case, one party, usually the patient, may show a premature inclination to stop treatment. It is recommended that the therapist consider ways of dealing with such inclinations, especially through understanding the transference.

4. Having achieved the goals, the patient and therapist begin to worry whether the achievement can be maintained, whether the separation can be managed, and whether the patient is really ready for termination. It is recommended that the therapist will have taken up previous separations and will recognize the resurgence of symptoms as a way of dealing with the meaning of termination.

5. The patient and therapist consider the question of further contact after termination. It is recommended that the therapist allow for further contact and deal with the need for further treatment if necessary.

Reclarifying the Time Structure

In the time-open-ended form of supportive–expressive psychotherapy (SE-TO) it is helpful to clarify in the beginning how the length of treatment will be decided. The therapist may say: "The length of the treatment is open-ended. It means that we will continue until you come to a point where you are satisfied with the changes you have made. It may take a few months or many months; we will decide what is best as we go along."

For time-limited psychotherapy (SE-TL), if the patient is told at the beginning on at least two occasions about the length of treatment, the problems faced by patient and therapist in dealing with the eventual termination will be minimized. This recommendation is appropriate for time-limited treatments since some patients are inclined to "forget" the initial instruction about the time limitation. A clear statement at the outset will minimize the possible sense of rejection about the time limit and will make it easier for the patient to prepare to separate at the end. Time-limited treatment can produce significant benefits for the patient, and it will help the therapist in dealing with the termination to know that. These benefits are usually not significantly less than those in time-unlimited treatment (if one can credit the available studies, as reviewed by Luborsky, Singer, and Luborsky 1975). Furthermore, when the treatment is sufficiently structured at the outset as time limited, patients go through all the phases of the longer treatment in the more condensed time period and are less prone to experience the treatment as being abruptly or unfairly cut off. Since the patient and therapist understand the time perspective in advance of and throughout treatment, much of what would occur in a longer treatment gets shaped by the time interval so that the treatment still contains a beginning, middle, and end. If the patient does not speak spontaneously of termination, even though it is approaching, the therapist should find out whether the patient is responding to termination but not speaking about it.

Noting Cues About the Patient's Conditions for Termination

The context in which the patient mentions the idea of cutting down on treatment or terminating, even when termination is not seriously being considered, often provides important cues about the patient's conditions for termination. The topic the patient is talking about at the moment the possibility of termination is broached tends to be one which, if the topic were further worked through, would enable the patient to terminate. A comment from the therapist to that effect is sometimes indicated.

EXAMPLE: Mr. T. G.
   P: I am feeling good about myself now because of my success on the job. Maybe I can begin to think about cutting down from two sessions per week to one.
   T: Getting that good feeling about yourself is so crucial that when you find ways to achieve it, you can begin to think of being closer to finishing the treatment.

When he spoke about reducing the number of sessions, the patient had been talking about his having achieved a better level of self-esteem. It is that topic which, if worked through further, would permit the patient to terminate. For this patient, where the treatment required constant attention to the focal goal, the talk of termination served the useful purpose of communicating to the therapist the connection between reaching his goal and cutting down on the sessions.

Marking Treatment Phases So They Serve as Milestones

Throughout the treatment, the therapist should be alert to end-phases within the treatment in relation to the achievement of the patient's goals, as Schlesinger (1977) has pointed out. This principle is especially true for the brief SE-TL. It is of special value for therapist and patient to notice the completion, or even partial completion of goals and the setting of new ones. Marking such milestones provides a sense of completion and progress to the patient at a level which is readily understandable (as noted under the beginning phase, chapter 5). It can also provide a brake on too much unreflective involvement in the transference relationship in which the patient too completely believes the experienced current relationship is the actual current relationship.

An example from a treatment will show how a focus upon beginnings and endings of phases in relation to goals is beneficial and, furthermore, can be thought of as a gradual process of refined diagnosis of the patient's problems.

EXAMPLE: Mr. F.

The patient was near the last month of a year-long treatment in which he had been gradually coming to see the main theme of his principal area of vulnerability. He had a paranoid sensitivity to the imputation of nonmanliness. For most of the treatment the essence of the patient's main theme had been, "I want to feel I'm okay," in the sense of being manly, "but I'm constantly undercut." In the session previous to the current supervision hour, the patient had clearly indicated that he was experiencing considerable identification and camaraderie with the therapist. He now felt he had come to a level of functioning that was much closer to his goal. For example, he said: "I got the music fellowship and I got the money for it." He recounted having his first experience of sleeping with his new girl friend, and then concluded, "It was good. My relationships are getting better. The only thing I want is to move closer to people. I want to be closer with you, too. In fact, I'd like you and your wife to go with me and my girl friend to a movie and music."

In terms of Schlesinger's views (1977), this juncture can be partially understood as a completion of a phase in the sense of the patient having a more satisfactory solution to his goal of feeling more manly and consequently less vulnerable to the imputation of nonmanliness. He felt he was achieving this, both with the opposite sex and with work.

In the supervision, the supervisor suggested that the therapist review with the patient the fact that the patient had fulfilled his main agenda in treatment and was now raising a remaining goal. Then the therapist should listen to the patient's response to that and in that way try to understand the meaning of the patient's request. The patient was implying but not stating, (in essence) "I'm not undercut in my masculinity now. I think I can avoid that experience if you [the therapist] maintain social contact with me." That may then be the main meaning that may need to be reviewed with the patient: that he feels a social contact with the therapist will put a seal on his feelings of manliness. A related meaning of the new goal of maintaining contact with the therapist after treatment may have been to hold onto the gains of treatment by lessening the experience of separation. In any case, the main point of the suggested technique would be to explore the meaning of the patient's having essentially said he completed his goal and then added a provision containing a possible new goal.

Recognizing the "Arrival" at Termination in Terms of Goals Having Been Reached

The arrival at a satisfactory position of achievement of the initial treatment goals is a natural basis for considering termination. A satisfactory position means that the symptoms and related suffering are lessened to a point where they are less urgent or even absent. Recognition of this happy state by the patient and therapist should occur at such times.

Yet this arrival by itself is not a sufficient condition for termination. To go ahead with termination, the patient must decide that no new goals are worthy of further work in the treatment. Most crucially, the patient must be ready to deal with the separation from the therapist. Working through the meaning of separation means that the gains can be maintained. If that readiness is not strong enough the patient may discover new goals which are brought forward as a basis for extending the treatment. In that case, the difficulty of dealing with the separation should become the focus of the treatment.

EXAMPLE: Ms. L. H.

The example shows the patient had become increasingly ready to deal with setting a time to terminate and that readiness had been partly based on the achievement of her goal of stopping uncontrollable bouts of eating followed by vomiting (bulimia). She was further fortified in feeling ready by the way she was dealing with the meaning of termination, as shown in her dream. In the dream she sees herself as maintaining contact with the therapist and getting recognition from her [the therapist] because she [the patient] has also become a professional woman in the same field and even manages in the dream to elicit information from a patient which the therapist had missed.

P: I'm amazed at the way I'm handling things. It's wonderful! And I'm in school plus I helped Sis go to the hospital for her operation. . . . There are a lot of these things and yet I'm fine, totally fine. What's interesting is I keep thinking how we've talked about how maybe soon I'll stop seeing you and shortly after I had this dream:

I don't know if I was coming to see you in a session or just coming to visit you, but I was in the same room with you. You were not very far away. The room was not big. You were talking with a woman who was mentally ill. She reminded me of a woman I saw in the emergency room a couple of weeks ago. She said, "I need help." You were speaking low so I didn't hear it. You were called away to a phone call which ended the session with the woman. She didn't leave and told me to have a seat. She started talking to me about how she needed help and told me about her problems. She left. You returned. Again I'm not sure if I was there for a session or visit but it turned into a discussion about this woman's case. You shared with me your observations and I told you what she told me.

It's significant for me because I guess I'm not seeing you as my therapist or having my need to come to treatment.

T: What do you make of the dream?

P: I'm thinking of not coming a lot and in it I saw you on a more professional level. I'm going into the field. I was seeing you as a professional rather than my therapist.

T: The dream expresses the natural wish to have a different kind of relationship. If you're leaving treatment, we won't see each other anymore so there is the wish for a different type of relationship.

P: I have thought if I stop what happens then? Will I be able to see you in a couple of months or a year just to keep you up to date. Not because I'm slipping back. That's not the fear. Just to keep in contact.

T: I'd always like to hear from you and how you're doing.

P: I'd really like to have a phone number. It would represent security. Just in case. Not that I'm anticipating it. I would just wanna reach out.

T: (Gave patient her office phone number) They'll always know where I'll be. I'd love to hear from you.

P: I'm not even that afraid of going off by myself because these two weeks have been stressful and I can handle it. I'm feeling better about myself. I'm taking better care of myself. I can't believe a year ago I was so obsessed with food, though I still like to eat! I think of it in a relative way.

EXAMPLE: Mrs. L.

The following example is one where achievement of the goals nearly precipitated termination but then new goals appeared which justified continuation of the treatment.

After about two years of twice-a-week treatment in which the initial goal was primarily to find ways to overcome an almost lifelong proneness to severe depression, the patient began to consider termination because for the past nine months no depression had been present and, even more, she felt a consistent sense of effectiveness in her work. The patient and therapist both recognized this milestone. The dramatic lessening in proneness to depression came about through working out her fear of competition with her sister, parents, and with the therapist. The relationship problem was still evident after the nine-month period of freedom from major depressions but also there were improved ways of mastering it through being able to show assertiveness. After seriously considering termination, a new treatment phase was begun with a limited related goal.

Achieving Goals Does Not Mean the Relationship Problems Are All Gone

The typical improvements achieved by the end of psychotherapy are in (a) the target symptoms, that is, the initially stated complaints, and in (b) the relationship theme which is the usual context for the symptoms. Patients tend to come to a point where they feel a reasonable achievement of the goals has been made, although all the goals have not been realized. The symptoms are more likely to have been changed than the relationship problems.

By the end of treatment, the initial relationship problems still tend to be recognizable but fortunately with an important addition—a greater sense of mastery over them. Research on the core conflictual relationship theme method has given support to this conclusion (Luborsky 1977): A comparison of more versus less improved patients showed that the CCRT was present both early and late in treatment for both the more and less improved patients. The important difference between the two groups, however, was that the more improved patients showed a greater sense of mastery of the relationship problems in the theme.

The following example (as well as the previous example for Mrs. L.) illustrates this point.

EXAMPLE: Mr. Q.

The primary goal of the treatment was to reduce the proneness to severe depression. The CCRT described earlier revealed a sense of severe inadequacy in comparison with other men so that whenever the patient felt angry, he would be inclined to become depressed, often because of his estimate of his relative inadequacy. By the end of treatment, he had achieved more in his work, had gotten married, and had achieved a considerable lessening of his inadequacy feelings. Consequently he had gotten better control over his depressions, which had become much less frequent and less severe. There were times in which he felt the same inadequacy and anger at men, but he now had greater ability to modulate his inclination toward feeling "bad" which, earlier, had been followed by being depressed. The patient therefore felt ready to terminate and the therapist was in accord.

Dealing with the Inclination to End the Treatment Prematurely

Some patients arrive at points in their psychotherapy when they feel they need to break off the treatment before the treatment is completed. Patients may explain such inclinations in terms of disillusionment with getting what is needed from the treatment, or equally often, on outside pressures that necessitate the stoppage of the treatment. Fortunately this impulse tends not to be acted on immediately.

At such times, the therapist's first hypotheses should be in the direction of understanding how this may have emerged from the relationship with the patient. The therapist may conclude that the patient's inclination to break off treatment is the result of involvement in a transference issue which the patient finds too difficult to cope with. When the therapist deals with the transference issue directly, typically it has a mending-of-the-relationship effect and the threat to the treatment is diminished, with a vital gain in understanding by the patient and therapist.

Yet sometimes such transference interpretation does not work and the therapist is forced to conclude that his or her best efforts at these interpretations have not had their intended effect in easing the pressure toward premature termination. The therapist may then decide that a direct response to the patient's need either in terms of lessening the transference bind or in terms of lessening the patient's external pressure may be in order (as in the example below where the therapist offers the patient a special arrangement in terms of the scheduling of the session). On these occasions the therapist may try to ease the pressure on the patient in the most direct way possible, based on the logical principle that the therapist cannot treat a patient who is not there.

If premature termination still seems inevitable despite the two avenues suggested, the time for it should be set up several sessions in advance to allow the patient and therapist to review what has happened. Arranging for such a review period is much easier when a prearranged lead-in time has been discussed and agreed to at the beginning of the treatment as part of the ground rules of the treatment arrangements. The therapist should ask the patient that whenever termination is approaching, a certain interval of treatment be devoted to reviewing the treatment before the actual termination occurs.

EXAMPLE: Ms. B. D.
The patient said she felt extremely pressured and overwhelmed by the number of afterwork assignments she had

taken on. Under these circumstances coming to treatment was too much, especially treatment at the usual time. The therapist tried to show that she was willing to make the best possible time arrangement for the patient.

The therapist's response did not adequately deal with the transference issue which had been partly stimulated by the therapist. The therapist had not recognized that she had contributed to the patient's pressure in the previous session by not responding to the patient's need for support when the patient had revealed her overwhelmingly frightening physical problems. The patient had described the kind of pressure she had experienced when her mother would not be supportive under similar circumstances. A transference interpretation, which also recognized the therapist's behavior, might have eased the patient's overload and consequent readiness to bolt the treatment.

Dealing with Previous Separations Eases the Termination

Experience with reactions to separations prepares the patient for termination (Edelson 1963). It is hard to do all the work of termination without some of that preparation; it is almost too late if termination is the first such experience in the treatment.

Fortunately, life being what it is, occasional opportunities occur, such as vacations, meetings, and illnesses. The working through of the meaning of these separations need not be profound. Minimally, all the patient may recognize is that the separation is being responded to. How it is responded to varies but includes some frequent forms: anger and impulses to retaliation, loneliness and feelings of desertion, and signs of increased distance. One evidence of distance, to be discussed next, is the loss of the treatment gains and the return of the symptoms.

Recognizing the Resurgence of Symptoms as a Way of Dealing with the Meanings of Termination

In both SE and SE-TL, it is usual to find a period of resurgence of initial problems at the time the termination is approaching. If this revival of symptoms is reviewed with the patient in terms of its meaning in relation to ending, the surge usually subsides and there is more chance of the patient's reclaiming the gains that had been made earlier. One of the frequent meanings of the renewed symptoms is that without the continued presence of the therapist, the patient expects to revert to the pretreatment state. It is as if the patient forgets that the gains that had been made reflect changes that came about through the patient's participation. The gains do not depend upon the continued physical presence of the therapist since the patient has now internalized some of the tools which the patient and therapist have used together. In fact, the patient can also be reminded that the process of change instilled by the treatment does not stop with the termination but continues on.

EXAMPLE: Ms. L. H. (see also pp. 148–150.)
   P: Yesterday it got so wet it was really dangerous to ride my bike. I don't know what I'm going to do in the wintertime. What's worst is when it's really wet and you can't see the puddles. Water fills the potholes and you can't see 'em. . . . My expectations of myself are much more realistic now. I don't thrash myself if I don't get

everything done. I'm setting more realistic short-term goals and meeting them.

T: Last time when we talked about goals self-regulation was your biggest goal.

P: Yeah, I do fall back into it. But I'm progressing and feeling good about that. There's something really bugging me, though. I wanted to bring it up—basically, it's that need to take in. The first week I didn't see you everything went fine. The second week I slipped into eating more than I liked. I have to realize I need to eat sometimes, so I allow myself an extra piece of cake. But I do reproach myself and feel I'm bad. Two times this week I felt the urge to take in laxatives because I felt I'd overeaten . . . yet I didn't take them. Bothered me the feeling was so strong, and yet I had it after not having it for so long. Here I was thinking this was going to be my last session with you and now I've had this feeling. I don't know that I can deal with it. I don't want to cling to you and yet that feeling was so strong . . . .

T: Your pattern we talked about is to rigidly control to prevent going all the way. You're experiencing the renewed fear that if you take one more cup of coffee or one more piece of cake you will be out of control. You haven't had that feeling for a while.

P: I have to remind myself that it is sometimes okay to feel full. I went to a lovely dinner this weekend. A mutual friend is into gourmet cooking. I haven't felt that stuffed in years. I didn't feel good. I was a pig. Why did I do that? I have to remind myself that people do it on special occasions. They survive. But I can't seem to eat to enjoy myself all the time. Again I want to control myself better.

T: Perhaps one reason you're having a resurgence of the need for control is you've gotten used to seeing me as a helper. Now you're thinking of leaving treatment. I went away and you got a little panicky.

P: I overate all last week. Yesterday I controlled it. I have to eat breakfast. I seem to be more obsessed with weight these days. I have to watch it. Yesterday it was okay. I wonder if there is a correlation with how I'm seeing you.

T: You know, at the end of treatment there's often a resurgence of some of the original symptoms because of anxiety about leaving here.

P: Yes anxiety is there.

T: You talked of anxiety about losing your control but you have had control and still have the tools, as you have told me today.

P: Yes I know [she gave further examples of control with men and weight]. (P and T settled on another session before terminating.)

Allowing for Further Contact After Termination

Most patients are naturally interested in keeping up some form of contact with the therapist after treatment is over. "Naturally" is the right adjective, because if the relationship has been helpful, as most of them are, there is a positive attachment and therefore a sense of loss at giving up seeing the therapist. Consequently the patient is interested in the therapist's reactions to his or her wish for further contact. One way to find this out is to ask whether the therapist wants to be kept up-to-date on progress after termination. Unless the session indicates some other additional responses, the therapist may express what he or she usually feels, namely a wish to hear how things are going. Being reassured by such an exchange that contact is possible can contribute to the posttreatment maintenance of the treatment gains. It is often useful also to have a prearranged follow-up, such as a session or two within the six months following the last regularly scheduled session of the treatment.

The preceding example of Ms. L. H. reflects the resolution of the opposed wishes: complete the therapy versus avoidance of separation. That feat is accomplished by moving ahead toward termination but arranging for the possibility of future contacts. In the dream the feat is arranged by the patient's becoming a professional and in that way a colleague and a peer of the therapist. In fact, in her career training she is moving in that direction. She also arranged to get the therapist's phone number since it would serve "to keep you up-to-date" and "it would represent security."

Dealing with the Need for Further Treatment

In SE, if the goals are not met by the time of the intended termination, it is no special problem: an extension of the treatment is arranged. In SE-TL, at the time of the intended termination, if new goals are raised or the old goals are not achievable in the time remaining, an extension of time beyond the limit might be arranged. If there is a clinic regulation or research protocol that precludes it, a referral to another therapist would have to be set up.

10

Variations and Adjuncts

Four familiar variations and adjuncts will be discussed in this chapter: (1) Time-limited psychotherapy (SE-TL) can be an appropriate treatment variation for some patients. Its main defining characteristics will be reviewed along with one example of its application. (2) An occasionally necessary adjunct to both time-limited and time-open-ended psychotherapy is the expansion of the treatment group to include the family and other people who are involved with the patient. (3) An adjunct to both forms of treatment is the addition of psychotropic medication. (4) Lastly, a comprehensive physical examination should be routinely recommended before the start of psychotherapy.

Time-limited Psychotherapy (SE-TL)

Principles and directions for SE-TL have been given throughout the manual wherever they were appropriate to distinguish it from SE. The two main distinctive qualities of SE-TL are summed up here:

1. Time Limit. The crucial difference between SE and SE-TL is in the time limit and its consequences. Fixing that time limit has shaping effects throughout the treatment. In SE-TL the therapist and patient agree on the time limit, sometimes with a provision for a follow-up. The limit is usually less than 25 sessions.

2. Consistent Therapeutic Focus. Both treatment formats, the supportive–expressive therapy (SE) and the SE-TL are "focal psychotherapies" in that a selection is made early in the treatment of a primary goal around which the therapeutic work is to be concentrated. SE-TL has more of this concentration on a particular focus. Usually, the focus is on a facet of the core conflictual relationship theme (CCRT) and the symptoms connected with it. That facet is usually related to one of the patient's goals. In its concentration on a particular goal, SE-TL more than SE is in the lineage of short-term psychotherapies which include Balint (1972), Malan (1963, 1976), Sifneos (1972), and Mann (1973).

Aside from these two distinctive areas of difference between SE and SE-TL, the two treatments have major resemblances. For example, they are like each other in their temporal phases. SE-TL is organized and shaped by the time structure rather than being just a truncated SE treatment, so that it too has a definite beginning, middle, and end.

EXAMPLE: Mr. F. G.

This example illustrates many of the characteristics of SE-TL. These were considered by the therapist in coming to a decision to limit the treatment to 10 sessions. Some of the criteria were noted during the routine pretreatment evaluation

160

(and are given in more detail in the report of the evaluation in appendix 2):

1. The patient was highly motivated for treatment.
2. He understood that there was a large psychological contribution to his main symptom of depression.
3. He had functioned well all of his life until the depression six years earlier at the time of his mother's death when he had a period of psychotherapy.
4. He was inclined to become dependent and the time-limited treatment would be likely to limit that.

The pretreatment evaluation also led to some tentative decisions about the procedures in the intended treatment:

1. The treatment was to be supportive, which meant: (a) the therapist would recognize and in that way further the maintenance of his many areas of competence. (b) The therapist would explore the physical health problems to see how they intertwined with the psychological ones or were even direct expressions of the physical ones; for example, the impotence might be a manifestation of the depression and/or of the Inderal which was prescribed for the high blood pressure. In order to test the effect of the Inderal it was temporarily halted, after consultation with the internist.

2. The treatment was also to be expressive, which meant that the therapist would help the patient explore the meaning to the patient of the wife's lack of interest in sexual activity, of the boss's putting him down, and of his impotence. These factors, as well as his mother's death might have played a part in the onset and maintenance of the depression.

The treatment carried out the intended techniques and fulfilled the therapist's anticipations. The change in the Inderal was found to have no discernible effect on the impotence. The patient and the therapist formed a strong positive relationship from the beginning and the depression gradually diminished. Some renewal of the depression occurred at the sixth session. It seemed likely that the prospect of completing treatment and losing the therapist had scared the patient enough so that his symptoms began to return. Then, after the therapist reviewed the time arrangement with him and began to deal with the meaning of completing treatment, the depression again continued to reduce.

A portion of session 9 is given below for it shows in a lively way the nature of the relationship and the understandings the patient and therapist were able to achieve:

T: You must be back at work.

P: How do you know? Do I look tired?

T: No, the bandage is off.

P: I went back on Monday. This cut wasn't much. I think the doctor was mostly worried about infection and maybe he thought I needed a rest.

T: How is your hand?

P: It's fine. (He showed the therapist) The boss is on vacation for two weeks, that's good. I was off two weeks and now he's off two weeks, that's quite a vacation. Everybody in the shop is happy. (P and T laugh together) (silence) What's the matter?

This begins a discussion of the patient's readiness to react to the therapist's silence by upsetness, feeling rejected, and possibly eventually depression.

T; Let's talk about that. When I'm quiet do you really feel like something is wrong?

P: No, I feel left out, like you're studying something. Do you understand?

T: No.

P: When people don't talk, it is completely silent. I don't hear anything. It's like something else got their attention, and I don't know where it is. I look around. If they turn their heads, then I know I missed something.

T: But here if I'm quiet and look at you, how do you feel?

P: Like you notice something.

T: You mean you wonder how I think of you, like a patient, a real person, an experiment?

P: Yes.

T: You told me that Dr. N. (former therapist) didn't talk to you.

P: Yes, he didn't say anything, I just talked. When you go to the doctor, like if you have a broken arm, you say, "my arm is broken." You want them to do something. It's the same with a mental problem.

T; Sure, you say you have a problem and you want it fixed.

P: Yes.

T: In therapy, it's a little bit different because we try to help people discover the power of healing within themselves. So if somebody says what should I do about this or that problem, we don't try to give advice about what to do, because what's right for one person might not be the right solution for another, and we try to help each person find the right solution for themselves.

P: Agreed. . . .

T: Have you been thinking about the fact that we'll only have one more meeting?

P: Yes. Are you going to round it up? I don't have any depression anymore, but what will I do if it comes back? How will I get rid of it?

T: Well, what have you learned?

P: To understand it. Uh, sometimes people just talk to me and I don't say much and they say thanks for the help.

But I didn't do anything. I just listened. It helps. Somehow they figure it out.

T: You do that for people?

P: Uh-huh.

T: I'll bet you do more. Like they know they're not alone with their worry.

P: Not alone, that's very important. One thing though, I still can't concentrate and it's so important now. (The patient appeared to be considering presenting this as a new goal of the treatment and as a basis for extending the treatment.)

T: Yes. It kind of gets you in a bind because you worry about it and worrying makes it harder to concentrate. . . . There are lots of things like that in life, but when you relax a bit it gets easier. Like you told me about doing math problems step by step. You feel like you're running out of time, but really there is time to do everything that's important.

P: I told my wife there's not enough time to stay together just to be miserable. There's only two things to do. She said she loves me and her lack of desire for sex isn't because of me. It's because she hasn't had a period for a year. I told her to go to the doctor and she says she will.

(Note in the evaluation report the patient had thought the wife was still menstruating.)

T: She must be scared. She's 46. The usual reason a woman's period stops is the menopause. You didn't know about what your wife was feeling. It affects women in different ways. Sometimes they feel less of a woman. Then later they accept it and they feel more sexy because they know they won't get pregnant.

P: I can understand that.

T: Some people think they shouldn't have sex then, but it's
    not true. She should go to the doctor to make sure and
    get some information. She must be scared.

P: We had sex twice this week. It wasn't great, but it was
    okay. I think if she was warmer to me I could do better.
    What if she gets too sexy and I can't do enough?

T: I don't know what will happen, but now you two are
    talking about it with each other and I think you'll work
    it out when the time comes. See, you're saying you have
    two choices. To separate or renew your commitment to
    treasure each other. You're not telling me you want to
    get divorced and be alone. You wanted to make your
    home.

P: I don't want to get divorced. I ran around when I was
    young and the women did too. It's part of growing up but
    now I-I've grown up and I don't want to run around. . . .
    I've been wanting to ask you, with all the people you see,
    how do you remember all the, all those things? Do you
    have a tape recorder? (The patient appears to be think-
    ing that this has been a memorable relationship he has
    settled into with the therapist and he supposes it must be
    for her too and he wants her to acknowledge it).

T: No. Each patient is an individual. Just like you remem-
    ber things about people you know.

Several healing elements may have been responsible for the
benefits the patient achieved and some are evident in this
session. First and most essential, he felt understood and part
of a supportive relationship with the therapist. Next, the patient felt less impotent and more in control in the relationship
with the therapist than he did when the treatment started. The
therapist tried to let the patient realize that the power of
healing was in himself and not just in the therapist. Next the
patient felt emboldened to explore his wife's coldness, both

emotional and sexual, and as a consequence learned that it derived from her own physical problem and it was not therefore a reflection on him. His impotence virtually vanished and he began to resume a sexual life and felt less of a failure. The supportive relationship with the therapist as well as the improvement in the relationship with the wife helped in the recovery from the depression.

Family and Other Partners in the Treatment Group

SE is typically an individual psychotherapy. Much of its therapeutic leverage is delivered by means of developing and altering the relationship between the patient and therapist through understanding their relationship, particularly by analysis of the transference.

Yet this does not mean that SE must always be restricted to the patient and therapist alone. The patient almost always has some close family or family-like relationships and it is sometimes useful to have some sessions together with one or more members of these groups. Most often the groups comprise parents, siblings, spouse, or other partners. The sessions with the expanded group will provide special information from other vantage points and may also provide a critical potential for further therapeutic leverage:

1. The special information comes from the patient's and therapist's witnessing of the patient's interactions with the others and therefore understanding them better. Often the understanding is deepened by seeing the parallel with the patient–therapist interactions.

2. The further therapeutic power comes from the presence

of the other significant members of the patient's immediate group. Part of the power derives from the fact that (a) the other members of the group also form a treatment bond and are enlisted by the therapist as therapeutic change agents, and that (b) the expanded focus of therapeutic work is on changing the group structure. This basic idea of working therapeutically with the patient as part of a group of closely related people, deriving understanding from the structure of that group, and picking from it a focal target of therapeutic effort has been thoroughly and artfully presented by Minuchin (1974).

A recommended way of setting up the group treatment is to have the patient invite the others with the following introduction, which is then repeated by the therapist when the group first convenes:

T: We find it important to know how you see the patient's problems. We, therefore, want you to be present and take part. How do you see the problem?

Significant Other: (gives his or her views)

T asks P: Would you please say how you see the problem so that (other) can hear how you see it?

An exchange then will begin between the patient and the significant other person. After hearing the exchange the therapist will be in a position to evaluate the relationship problems between the two and can decide on a therapeutic strategy. An initial step is for the therapist to show both of them what their interaction is like. On the basis of their previous participation in the psychotherapy the therapist and patient usually are in a good position to see whether the relationship problems with the significant other are like the relationship problems with the therapist and the parents.

In about 1 out of 10 of the outpatient SE treatments, the use of this kind of expanded group as an adjunct to the SE individual psychotherapy seemed potentially helpful. For the rest, such an adjunct did not seem to be needed and the patients generally benefited as well without it.

EXAMPLE: Mrs. M. (see p. 99–100)

She was able after about a year of once-a-week individual psychotherapy to decide to ask her husband to come and join . her in the treatment. In the course of the next several months, the husband was invited about every other week. During this period, she was able to work out her own strategy for achieving a greater sense of freedom and, therefore, greater freedom from her sexual inhibition. Without the support provided to the husband by being made part of the therapy, it seems unlikely that he could have accepted her own strategy for freedom. The therapeutic leverage came from two factors: the patient felt able to express what she needed and the husband felt supported by being part of the therapeutic group. The successful conclusion of this therapy in terms of the resolution of the patient's initial symptoms might certainly have occurred without bringing in the husband, but that act seemed to facilitate a leap in progress and shortened the therapeutic work.

A somewhat less dramatic benefit was achieved in another patient who wanted to and did bring in her husband. After about six months of individual psychotherapy the patient wanted to bring in her husband to help make him a party to the solution of their sexual problems. The therapist agreed, the patient enlisted the husband, the patient and husband came in, and the therapist again explained the patient's need to have the husband join them. After several meetings, an added gain was noticed in terms of having enlisted the husband in helping toward the solution. In this second example, the gains were not as dramatic as in the first, but a definite therapeutic leverage was achieved.

Psychopharmacological Treatments Used in Combination with Psychotherapy

Psychopharmacological agents can be helpful when there is a clear indication for them. One of the main risks in terms of the psychotherapy is that psychopharmacological agents will be overused, that is, they will be used instead of reliance on psychotherapeutic techniques. When these agents are employed, their use should be consistent with these principles:

PRINCIPLES OF PSYCHOPHARMACOLOGY

Principle 1. Combined treatments consisting of psychopharmacological agents added to psychotherapy can be better than psychotherapy alone.
A considerable body of research shows that with some types of patients, adding pharmacological agents can assist the patient's progress. Knowledge in this field has grown rapidly and even expands noticeably from year to year (as reviewed by Luborsky, Mintz, Auerbach, Crits-Christoph, Bachrach, and Cohen 1984). In that review, of 15 studies, 12 showed a significant advantage for the combination versus psychotherapy alone. The other three showed a nonsignificant difference. Most of these studies used psychodynamically oriented psychotherapy which resembles SE, according to the brief descriptions in the studies. Although the studies tended to be weighted toward in-patients, especially schizophrenic patients, the studies with neurotic out-patients showed the same trend. Combination treatments seem

in general to be advantageous since two other combination treatments showed the same positive trend; these are: (a) psychotherapy plus pharmacotherapy versus pharmacotherapy alone, and, another highly effective one, (b) psychotherapy plus a medication regimen versus a medication regimen alone for psychosomatic illnesses.

Why should these treatment combinations be especially beneficial? They may represent just an additive effect or they may represent some mutually facilitative benefits. In a review by Smith, Glass, and Miller (1980, p. 180), combined treatments were shown to produce an effect size which is larger than either treatment effect size; however, the combination was largely additive rather than mutually facilitative. Similarly, in the four studies of tricyclic antidepressants in combination with psychotherapy as compared with either treatment alone, or no treatment, an additive effect was found for the treatment of ambulatory nonpsychotic nonbipolar moderately depressed patients (Weissman 1979).

Two options are available for dealing with prescribed medications in research studies: option 1 is to prescribe medications as needed by some patients. The hoped-for results of using this open-ended option are that (a) the groups being compared will get what they need in terms of necessary medications but will not, by the end, have different amounts of prescribed medications; or (b) if they do get different amounts, that the amount provided will not correlate with the main variables of the study. As an example of option 1, in the Penn Psychotherapy Project (Luborsky, Mintz, Auerbach, Christoph, Bachrach, Todd, Johnson, Cohen, and O'Brien 1980), the use versus non-use of medications had no relation to any of the outcome measures. Thirty-six percent of the 73 patients had some drugs prescribed during the course of the treatment. These were small to moderate doses of ataractics such as chlorodipoxide hydrochloride and diazepam, or antidepressants such as amitryptilene hydrochloride (Elavil).

Option 2 is to prescribe no medication for any patient. Option 2 is not used as often as option 1. It is more and more difficult to use option 2, since it may constitute depriving some patients of needed medications. When either option 1 or 2 is used, it is also necessary to keep a record of nonprescribed drugs taken by patients as well as a record of other psychological treatments received concurrently with the treatment, for example, counseling from a minister.

Principle 2. Therapists who are not qualified to provide psychopharmacotherapy should collaborate with a qualified professional.

Those therapists who are not knowledgeable about psychopharmacology or are not able legally to provide these agents might collaborate with a friendly expert; for example a psychiatrist who is experienced in this area. After prescribing the medication, the qualified professional can instruct the therapist about what to watch out for in terms of injurious side effects and other aspects of the treatment, or he or she may see the patient occasionally to provide this kind of supervision directly. With some patients, although the therapist has the knowledge to provide the medications, the therapist prefers to separate the medication giving from the psychotherapy giving functions. For example, as mentioned earlier, at the Menninger Foundation, for hospital patients it is a practice to assign each patient both a hospital doctor and a therapist, with the hospital doctor prescribing the medications and making other management decisions. Otherwise, if such collaboration for the provision of medications is not available, the therapist who is not qualified in this area should confine himself or herself to the large group of patients who do not or are not likely to need such medications.

Principle 3. The therapist should try to understand the meanings to the patient of the pharmacological agents.

The therapist should remember to attend to the meanings to the patient of the therapist's having arranged for medications and of the patient's taking medications (GAP 1975 and Docherty, Marder, Van Kammen, and Siris 1977.) Arranging for medications must constitute a significant intervention in relation to the patient. This principle is only an extention of the broader principle that the therapist should be aware of the meaning of his or her behavior in relation to the patient (Principle 7 of understanding). Some meanings may tie in with the patient's main relationship problems and may impede progress. Some of the usual meanings include (a) experiencing the taking of medication as a weakness and a giving up of self-control, (b) considering the recourse to taking medication as a sign of the failure of the psychotherapy, and (c) viewing the therapist as an extremely helpful or an omnipotent figure for having arranged for the magical medications.

Two more specific principles can be subsumed under the main principle:

Principle 3A. The therapist should identify to the patient the expected locus of action of the medication.

The function of this information, aside from the obvious one of keeping the patient informed about matters that are relevant, is to diminish the degree of misinterpretation about the aims and function of the medication. Typical targets of medication are to diminish irrational thinking or prevent its recurrence, or the reduction in depression or anxiety.

Principle 3B. The therapist should consider whether the medication is a substitute for dealing with a relationship problem between the patient and the therapist.

The heart of this principle is the necessity of determining whether the medication is being used to deal with a relationship problem that is amenable to psychotherapeutic means for its resolution. However, under some conditions the therapist may decide to use medication when, after careful evaluation, the conclusion is clear that psychotherapy alone will not be a viable approach even though a relationship problem is involved.

Physical Examinations

As a precautionary measure it is good to recommend a physical examination to all patients when they are about to start or have just started psychotherapy. In many settings this a routine part of the initial evaluation.

Some therapists may feel that a simpler course is to confine the patient's evaluation to the psychological sphere. Their justification could be that the patient has come for psychological help and therefore the physical evaluation can be left up to the patient and the patient's physicians. But that position could put some patients in jeopardy since the psychological sphere could reflect underlying physical disorders. Without a physical examination it is sometimes not clear to which patients this applies. Especially for patients with somatic and psychosomatic conditions, it is important that the patient and therapist either have ruled out or apportioned the relevant contribution of physical factors in relation to the psychological symptoms.

Two examples in this manual illustrate the benefits for the

psychotherapy of having a physical examination. The first is Mr. F.G. (p. 160) whose main symptom of depression was associated with impotence. The impotence could have been based on one of the side effects of the Inderal which the patient was taking for his blood pressure treatment. The physical examination showed that the Inderal was not the main contributor to the impotence. Another symptom, the confused states, could not be associated with any physical factors. This information was helpful in the psychotherapy to both the patient and the therapist. The effect was to clear up concerns about physical problems and also to allow attention to be redeployed onto the psychological problems.

Another patient, Mr. P., who had worrysome memory lapses was concerned that they might reflect organic brain disease. The physical evaluation with a special neuropsychology assessment indicated that the memory lapses were not evidence of brain disease. The information was a relief to the patient and permitted more attention to the psychological problems.

11

Analogic Summaries

This book would be ready for its termination now were it not for a new goal: the need to indulge in another mode of thinking on the nature of the listening, understanding and responding sequence, expressed as alternative analogies. The analogic mode of communication is an example of metaphoric thinking. It results in a more "primary process" based exposition rather than in the "secondary process" explanation used throughout this book. This mode conveys some of the therapist's experience of the treatment when engaging in the treatment. The experience of doing supportive-expressive (SE) treatment is captured in terms of any of these five analogies: nurturing an unfamiliar plant, peeling an onion, solving the crime in a mystery story, discerning a tree in a dense forest or playing a game of chess. The first one has more of a supportive flavor; the last four more of an expressive flavor.

Nurturing an Unfamiliar Plant

One vital analogy likens the process of psychotherapy to learning what is needed to cultivate under hot house conditions an unfamiliar plant which has had some growth problems. Since it is a living organism, it is safe to assume that it has growth potential. The conditions for facilitating this growth have to be found by attending to what makes it flourish and what makes it wither. Since it is a plant, one can make certain basic assumptions about its needs for light, water, air and nutrients —how much and what kind are to be learned by watching (listening for) its reaction as each condition is provided. Because the plant is in a hot house (the psychotherapy), many of the conditions for growth can be arranged. Since it has suffered certain growth problems, even all of the best performed ministrations may not correct all of them. But the safest attitude will be to keep on providing the best mix of nutrients (of the two main types, supportiveness and expressiveness) along with patient waiting and seeing. In summary, the provider provides, based on a general knowledge of plant care techniques, sharpened by exposure to the specific conditions for this plant, as well as by the wish to provide competent decent care.

Peeling an Onion

Each peeled layer reveals another; uncovering each one brings one closer to the core. The more closely one examines each layer, the more the eyes smart and the more likely it is that tears will be stimulated. But once the peeling is done, the tears can be brushed aside with the reflection that the result will form part of a reviving repast.

The analogy here with the process of psychotherapy is strong: each recognition of a current relationship problem as a layer of a revived emotion-laden past relationship problem can provide renewed strength to the patient (The principles of understanding and responding to the transference).

Solving the Crime in a Mystery Story

Another analogy likens the process to figuring out the culprit(s) in a mystery story.

Robert Waelder (1939) and Ekstein (1980), among others, used this simile for the interpretation process. The main requirement is that the patient and therapist (the pair of detectives) keep on the trail and follow the clues (the principles of understanding). The trail will lead to a clearer and clearer apprehension of "whodunnit." As in any good mystery, not all trails need to be followed in order to identify the culprit(s). In fact, one of the pleasures of a very good mystery story is the detective's clever inference-making that cuts through the tangle of overlapping or false clues and results in catching the perpetrators. The therapist and patient, like the detectives, only need to pursue the core and sufficient insights to achieve the desired results. Those mystery stories with the closest parallel to the SE version of psychotherapy rarely reveal a lone culprit. The "culprits" can be likened to the "guilty" relationship problems and related symptoms, and the factors that make them persist. The culprits typically did not do the dastardly deed only once, but repeatedly.

The detective-in-the-mystery-story analogy suggests some essential ingredients of this form of psychotherapy, yet it too has, or should have, its limits. The therapist must not become a relentless prosecutor, hunting down clues and, when he finds them, reacting with, "Ah hah, you have betrayed thus and so," so that the patient feels like a criminal.

Discerning a Tree in a Dense Forest

The process of understanding in psychotherapy is like gradually discerning the outlines of a tree (of meanings) in the midst of a dense forest (of possible meanings). The trunk is hard to see from a distance, but becomes unmistakable as one comes close to it. But some of the trunk and myriad branches remain mysteriously hidden, even when one is touching the tree trunk. In such a forest it is never possible to see the whole tree, either from a distance or close up, only repeated sightings from different perspectives will give the general gestalt, while some parts may remain forever hidden.

To climb down from the tree to the treatment, the crucial measure of how much one needs to uncover is based on the principle of uncovering as much as is necessary for each patient's recovery. For recovery to occur, therefore, seeing the whole tree is not essential; only enough of it needs to be exposed to deal with the relationship problems (branches) that are most in the way and bar progress (principle 6 of Understanding). The trunk of the tree might be the wishes, and the branches might be the consequences as organized in the core conflictual relationship theme method. When the patient and therapist focus on a particular relationship problem which is also seen in the current treatment relationship, connecting branches come into view that suggest hitherto unseen sources and possible problem solutions. After a sample of trunk and connecting branches has been uncovered and reviewed, the memory of all of them does not have to be retained by the patient. Rather, the crucial issue is whether the uncovering has permitted some of the possible problem solutions (principle 6 of Responding) to become part of the patient's behavior as modes of mastery.

Playing a Chess Game (Revisited)

Psychotherapy is like a chess game played out between the patient and the therapist. The fit of this analogy to the process of psychotherapy, noted at the beginning of this book, has become well known through Freud's (1913a) use of it. In a chess game, he observed, like psychotherapy, the rules for the opening and closing moves can be well specified but the rules for the intervening moves cannot be. These moves can be learned best by replaying the games of master players.

An apprentice system, since it allows for such exposure, is needed for learning both "games" and manuals can assist that system. However, for the kind of psychotherapy specified in this manual the analogy applies not only to opening and closing but to intervening moves as well. The manual offers rules that provide the therapist with an objective basis for interpretive responses at any stage of the game. These rules are based on the principle of recurrent focus on the CCRT (the first principle of understanding and of responding). Furthermore, the patient plays not just to win against the therapist, as would be true in a chess game, but also to form an alliance with the therapist so as to collaborate in finding how the patient's game has been self-hurtful and requires change. Collaboration is needed since the patient is not aware of, and even defended against knowing some of the fundamental rules by which he has been playing.

All of these five analogies can be seen to have metaphorically conveyed a piece of the therapeutic action but no one of them displays the whole action of supportive-expressive psychoanalytically oriented psychotherapy.

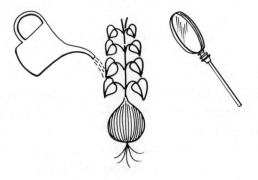

PART III

Appendices

Appendix 1

A Reminder Checklist for the Therapist for SE Treatment Arrangements

————Before treatment, arrange for the patient to have a pretreatment anticipatory socialization interview by a clinic agent, or for private practice, by some specially instructed referral sources (chapter 4).

————Before treatment, arrange for some participation in the choice process by patient and therapist (chapter 4).

————In the first session, discuss the main arrangements for the treatment, including number of sessions, whether time-open-ended or time-limited, fee, policy for missed appointments, and arrangements when termination is considered, et cetera (chapter 5).

————In the first session or two, decide with the patient on the main goals (to be rediscussed from time to time during the treatment) (chapter 5).

————In the early sessions and thereafter, formulate the main focus in terms of relationship problems (chapters 5, 7, and 8).

————As the treatment progresses, decide on the balance of supportiveness versus expressiveness (chapter 6).

————Prepare for termination well before it arrives. For example, (1) when short-term goals have been achieved, "mark" them with the patient; (2) allow sufficient time to work through the meaning of termination in order to optimize the retention of the gains (chapter 9).

Appendix 2

A Sample Report of a Pretreatment Diagnostic Evaluation Which Led to Time-Limited Psychotherapy

This summary was written on the basis of a pretreatment evaluation. Through this evaluation the therapist decided that the most appropriate treatment was to be time-limited (SE-TL as described in chapter 10).

Diagnostic Evaluation Summary

Mr. G.	60	
Patient's Name	Age	Date of Evaluation

IDENTIFYING DATA: Black male, married, employed full-time as a machinist

Baptist background with no church affiliation

CHIEF COMPLAINT: "Fits of depression."

HISTORY OF THE PRESENT ILLNESS: The patient was referred by Dr. A. from medical clinic for evaluation of depression. The patient stated that he has been prone to "fits of depression" for about five years. These periods last one-half to one day and are marked by a feeling of emptiness and lack of interest. He generally feels dazed and occasionally experiences throbbing temples. He believes "something is wrong," and questions whether it could be his medication but has no fear of serious organic illness such as cancer. He sleeps from 11 P.M. to 6 A.M. but has difficulty falling asleep and wakens unrested. He denies nightmares. He drinks about 1 pint of whiskey on weekends, but denies drinking during the week.

The patient works five days per week as a machinist and complained of working "not up to par" and making mistakes due to forgetfulness. He also complains of difficulty retaining leisure reading material.

He complained of being "impotent" with partial erections for five years. He has not attempted intercourse for the past two months because of "lack of confidence." He is scheduled to have an impotence evaluation. A penile prosthesis was recommended in the past.

An additional area of concern was his anticipated retirement. He thinks he should be developing interests such as photography in anticipation, but has not been motivated to do so.

The patient stated that he had previously been seen by a psychiatrist, Dr. N., in our OPD "years ago."

A review of available records indicates that Mr. G. received out-patient psychotherapy for approximately three months in

1976 for "chronic depression" and stopped for reasons which are unclear. At present the patient does not reveal his feelings about previous therapy other than to note that the therapist "never said anything." He seems to have an ambivalent attitude toward therapy now and has not revealed to his wife that he has come for evaluation.

A review of medical records from 1978 to the present time shows that the patient began taking hydrochlorthiazide and Inderal for hypertension in 1979. The first mention of impotence, fatigue, listlessness, and insomnia occurs in 4/4/81–10/81. He was given a trial off Inderal from 12/81–3/82 and the patient was apparently depressed in 3/82 when Inderal was restarted at 80 milligrams per day.

The patient was unable to associate any life events with the onset of depression. However, several events seem noteworthy: the patient's mother died in her 80s in 1976. She had suffered from severe dementia for two years prior to her death. The patient became tearful as he talked about her failure to recognize him, and his worry about the care his sister, an alcoholic, had given his mother during her last years. The patient is the seventh, and youngest child in his family and seems to have felt very close to his mother.

Secondly, a brother, now 65 years old has been "withdrawn from the world and confused" for about 10 years and is cared for by a sister. Mr. G. seems to be wondering whether he will become like this brother. Third, in 1976 or '77, a new foreman took over Mr. G.'s supervision at work. The foreman, now 57 years old, had been demoted from two positions at the manufacturing plant and is described as arbitrary, a petty stickler for rules, "has to be right," and chronically threatened and angry. Mr. G. believes that he takes much of the brunt of this man's action, as compared with the other machinists who are in their

30s and 40s. Until two years ago when his friend B. was able to obtain a transfer to another department, Mr. G. shared this role with B. and felt less vulnerable himself. His present thoughts about early retirement seem based solely on the wish to escape from the foreman and clearly not on a wish to stop working. His efforts to obtain transfers and seek fair work conditions through the labor union have been fruitless, and the patient feels impotent to change his job situation. He expressed his anger appropriately.

PERSONAL, FAMILY, AND SOCIAL HISTORY: The patient is the youngest of seven children, though two sisters died in youth from "childhood disease" and motor vehicle accident. As mentioned, a 65-year-old brother seems to have dementia, the oldest brother has diabetes, one sister has long been an alcoholic, the other living sister is not known to have health problems. The patient's father was in his 80s when he died with diabetes in 1949 (patient age 25), and his mother died in 1976 with dementia. The patient was raised in an intact family, graduated from junior high, and "dropped out" of vocational school. He fathered one child out of wedlock and was not involved in her rearing. She is now 41 years old. He has been married for 15 years and has two stepdaughters ages 27 and 24, who live elsewhere. He married "to have a home" and states that he has a "good" relationship with his wife who is 46 years old, and works full-time. The wife is premenopausal but Mr. G. does not feel she makes excessive sexual demands on him. The couple own their own house.

Mr. G. has held his job for 20 years. He noted that he lacks seniority over most of the younger men he works with.

MENTAL STATUS EXAM: The patient was a neatly groomed, alert, cooperative, and verbal 60-year-old plump male. There was

188

mild psychomotor retardation. Speech was slightly dysarthric. Thought processes were normal range and content revealed no delusions, paranoia, or suicidal ideation. Mood was "depressed." Affect was appropriate and of normal range with engaging social smile. Cognitive functions as indicated by modified Jacobs exam were excellent with rapid and correct performance and ready understanding of directions. Mild distraction was indicated by giving the date as the 15th and coming to his appointment at 10:45 instead of 10:15 as scheduled. This man appears to be of at least average intelligence though proverb interpretation was concrete. His judgment and insight are good.

CURRENT MEDICATIONS: Insulin (1957); Motrin 400 milligrams bid; Hydrodiuril 50 milligram bid 9/78; Inderal 40 milligram bid, 4/79; Sorbitrate 10 milligram; and Restoril 30 milligram hs.

IMPRESSION:

Axis I 300.40 Dysthymic Disorder

Axis II   None

Axis III
1. Diabetes Mellitus—on Insulin since 1957
2. Hypertension
3. Peripherial Vascular Disease s/p bilateral fem-pop bypass
4. Hard of hearing secondary to chronic mastoiditis and chronic otitis media, uses hearing aid
5. Degenerative Joint Disease—cervical spine
6. S/P Hepatitis
7. History Syphilis treated with penicillin

8. Impotence
Rule out neurologic or circulatory problems secondary to diabetes
Rule out medication side effect of Inderal
Rule out Depression
Rule out Marital problems
Rule out Alcohol

Axis IV   Code 3—mild—Disagreements with job foreman and anticipation of retirement

Axis V   Highest level of function past year—level 4 —fair—has trouble carrying out work assignments; increasing social withdrawal.

FORMULATION: This 60-year-old man with multiple medical problems presents with chronic depression and impotence. The onset and continuance of depression appear to parallel losses of physical health and important relationships with his mother (through death) and a co-worker/friend (through other's job transfer). He manifests mild anxiety and significant anger resulting from inability to improve a work situation in which he feels impotent. There is no obvious intellectual impairment.

At this time little is known of his early life as youngest child in a large family. His adult development is marked by rather late establishment of a stable marital relationship and career consolidation. At this time there is little evidence of mastery of Erikson's stage of generativity and marked despair over issues associated with aging, which may be related to identification with family members who have suffered from diabetes, dementia, and alcoholism.

PLAN: The patient gave verbal consent for me to obtain his medical records through his internist Dr. A.. It is noted that recent thyroid function tests were normal and no additional studies are recommended. Results of urologic impotence evaluation are pending. Dr. A. has agreed to a trial off Inderal and change of hypertension medication.

Mr. G. agrees to enter once-per-week psychotherapy with me for ten sessions. The emphasis will be on supportive-expressive intervention.

Appendix 3

An Anticipatory Socialization
Interview for Psychotherapy*

The two excerpts that follow are from a hypothetical anticipatory socialization interview developed by Orne and Wender(1968). The interview is preceded by taking a brief history of the patient's presenting complaint and circumstances surrounding it. That information helps to focus discussion by the interviewer and the patient on issues relevant to the particular patient and to provide for the interviewer meaningful illustrations based on the history. The interview is intended to be carried out by whoever is assigned to orient the patient to psychotherapy. During the first few sessions some of the points might well be restated by the therapist. Although the hypothetical interview is presented here as a monologue on the part of the interviewer, in actual practice it is interrupted by ques-

---

*A more extensive example of a hypothetical socialization interview has been deposited with the American Documentation Institute Auxiliary Publications Project, Photoduplicating Service, Library of Congress, Washington, D. C. 20540. It may be ordered by citing Document No. 9678 and remitting $1.75 for 35-mm microfilm or $2.50 for photoprints. Make checks payable to: Chief, Photoduplication Service, Library of Congress.

tions, amplified to clarify particular points, and varied to suit the particular case. An interview of this kind must be tailored to the specific therapist, patient, and the situation.

The major issues relevant for preliminary socialization for psychotherapy are taken up in this interview. The first excerpt below deals with the role of the patient in therapy. Here, what is conveyed is that it is the patient who will do most of the talking, while the therapist will do less. The patient learns also that the therapist will not give advice. Instead it is the patient who will learn to solve the problems. The interview strongly emphasizes the central role of curative factor # 1: the therapist will try to understand the patient; the patient will become aware of issues that were not known before. The new knowledge will include the unconscious operations of transference; the patient will be prepared especially for the appearance of the usual forms of negative transference. The interview ends with explanations about the value of following the instruction to try to say what the patient is thinking. The interview follows:

"Now, what is therapy about? What is going on? Well, for one thing, I have been talking a great deal; in treatment your therapist won't talk very much. The reason I am talking now is that I want to explain these things to you. There is an equally good reason that the therapist in treatment does not say much. Everyone expects to tell the therapist about his or her problem and then have the therapist give advice which will solve everything just like that. This isn't true; it just doesn't work like that. Advice is cheap; there is no reason to pay for it. Before you came here you got advice from all kinds of people: your spouse, your parents, your friends, your family doctor, your minister, and so on. Many of these people know you quite well; some of them know you very well; and if it were just a question of getting advice there is no reason to think that your therapist would be that much better at it than all of the people who have always told you what to do. Actually, we find that most people have a pretty good idea of what is wrong and while we can give advice to someone else with a problem similar to our own, it just doesn't help them. Unfortunately, when people give advice, they usually provide solutions which will work for themselves but not for the person who has the problem. If all of the advice you have received had helped, odds are that you wouldn't be here. Your therapist wants to help you to figure out what you really want to do—what the best solution is for you. It's the therapist's job not to give advice but to help you find out for yourself how you are going to solve your problems.

What does this mean? Well, if your therapist sees you getting into some kind of trouble, he or she may warn you about it, but here again the final decision as to what to do will have to be made by you. The great advantage you will have with your therapist is that he or she has no ax to grind. The therapist doesn't think he or she knows what is best for you, but is going to help you try to find out. The therapist doesn't think that he or she knows the answers but rather, he or she just wants to understand, with you, why you do things.

Now, what goes on in treatment itself? What is it that you talk about? What is it that you do? How does it work? Well, for one thing, you will talk about your wishes, needs, and intentions, both now and in the past. Why should this help? Why is it important? Well, there are many reasons. Ordinarily, people don't talk about lots of things because they are too personal, or because they would hurt other people's feelings, or for some other similar reasons. You will find that with your therapist you will be able to talk about anything that comes to your mind. He or she won't have any preconceived notions about what is right or what is wrong for you or what the best solution would be. Talking is very important because the therapist wants to help you get at what *you* really want. The problem most people have in making decisions is not that they don't know enough, but that they never have had the opportunity of talking things over with someone who doesn't try to make their decisions for them. The therapist's job is to help *you* make the decision.

Another reason is that most of us are not honest with ourselves. We try to kid ourselves, and it's your therapist's job to make you aware of when you are kidding yourself. The therapist is not going to try to tell you what he or she thinks but will point out to you how two things you are saying just don't fit together. You know, feelings have to add up, kind of like two and two are four, but we like to kid ourselves sometimes that they are five. It's your therapist's job to remind you when you are doing this. For example, let's take your ambivalence toward your wife (or parents). You have told me a lot of things you dislike about your wife—how annoyed you are with her, how you would sometimes like to leave her. But there are also reasons for continuing to live with her. There must be, because this is just what you are doing. The job of your doctor is to help you keep in mind all of the important facts and feelings so that you can come to a solution that takes all of the facts into account. It's hard because sometimes these feelings conflict; then again, if it were not hard you would not be here, you would not have the problems you do.

You have probably heard that therapists are interested in the subconscious. What is really meant by that? The subconscious isn't such a mysterious thing when one looks at it. For example, you must have met people who seem to get your goat and get you really angry with them, but you can't put your finger on anything they have done to account for your feelings. It may be that this person reminds you of someone but you don't realize it. The person whom he or she reminds you of is someone with whom you are angry, so you find yourself taking it out

195

on the person at hand. Unless you can remember whom you really are angry at, it's pretty hard to get over the feeling of annoyance. In this case, becoming aware of what is unconscious would be no more than remembering and recognizing the difference between these two people. Sometimes, though, that is an awful lot of work.

When we are not aware of the reason for a strong feeling like this, a therapist might then say this is unconscious. By becoming aware of the reasons for our anger with someone, we can treat him or her on a more realistic basis. It is easily possible that a very nice individual happens to resemble somebody whom we have good reason to dislike, and so we deprive ourselves of knowing somebody whom we would like because we are not aware of the resemblance. It is the therapist's job to help you recognize when the feelings you have toward someone seem to be inappropriate and then learn to understand the real causes. . . ."

A particularly important aspect of the interview relates to the discussion of negative transference and warning the patient of its consequences, thereby minimizing its potential for disrupting treatment.

"By the way, when you start in treatment, you will find that some of the people closest to you, who are for your getting some help now, may come to feel that it isn't helping you any. This is often an indication that you are changing, and these very changes are puzzling and troublesome to someone close to you. You should know that almost always in treatment some of the people around the patient will be convinced that he or she is getting worse—often just at the time when the patient is really improving. And you yourself might also sometimes feel worse and discouraged at some stages of treatment. You know, you'll feel you're not getting anywhere, your therapist doesn't know what he or she is doing, and there's no point in this, and so on. These very feelings are often good indications that you are working and that it's uncomfortable. It is very important that you don't give in to these temporary feelings when they come up.

You know, it's very funny—what will happen, as you talk about more difficult things, is that you'll find you have trouble keeping your appointments. You won't be able to get away from work, there will suddenly be necessary overtime just at the time of the appointment, your car will break down or run out of gas, your family will need your help at home for something, and so on. All of these things will seem quite unrelated to treatment. The funny part is that they'll be happening just at the time when things are getting rough for you in therapy. What this means, of course, is that you are getting down to something difficult and important, and that these are the most important times to bring yourself to your therapy meetings. This is something that always happens sooner or later. The only way to protect yourself is not to allow yourself to judge how important any given meeting will be, but instead to decide beforehand that you are going to be there, come hell or high water. In other words, if you make an appointment, you will keep the appointment regularly. This doesn't mean that you can't postpone a session for good reason, if you discuss it with your therapist beforehand. For example, if you know three or four weeks in advance that you've got a business trip, and you know it's something you have to do, it won't, as a rule, interfere with treatment if you miss an appointment. It's the sudden emergencies which are almost always unconsciously planned—things that come up unexpectedly.

Another thing—in treatment you will often find yourself uncomfortable. For one thing, your therapist won't say a great deal and you will find yourself trying to make decisions about what to say. We do this all the time. If we didn't, we would get ourselves into a lot of trouble. If you think your boss is an idiot and an s.o.b., and you told him this, you might well lose your job. In general, we have to make a distinction between what we think and what we say. In treatment this is not so. You want to say whatever comes to your mind, even if you think it is trivial or unimportant. It doesn't matter. It is still important to say it. And if you think it is going to bother your doctor, that doesn't matter either; you still say it. In contrast to your boss, if you think that your doctor is an idiot or an s.o.b., you need to tell him or her about it. You will find this is very hard to do and yet it is one of the most important things to learn in treatment—to talk about whatever comes to your mind. Often what you think is trivial and unimportant is really the key to something very important.

For example, you might suddenly become aware that the room is hot or that the doctor's clothes are funny or something like that which seems both trivial and even perhaps a little rude to bring up. Yet, in treatment, if you think of it, you say it. Many times I have seen things like this turn out to be extremely important. So, just like the appointments, we make an absolute rule that you should not think ahead about what you'll say and therefore protect yourself from facing important things. Say whatever is on the top of your mind, no matter what."

Appendix 4

An Example of the Core Conflictual Relationship Theme Method—Its Scoring and Research Supports

A good way to practice formulating the theme of the patient's core relationship problems is to review a series of "relationship episodes" selected from a patient's psychotherapy sessions. Relationship episodes are parts of sessions in which the patient offers a narrative of his or her interactions with other people, including with the therapist. The interactions with the therapist are sometimes more than narratives about the relationship with the therapist but are enactments of that relationship. For purposes of formulating the CCRT, concentrating on relationship episodes rather than on the whole session is economical and advantageous because the episodes give concrete examples of interactions with people in condensed form. The reader can come to a CCRT after reviewing the relationship episodes and scoring them following the principles below.

This appendix contains in order: the steps for scoring the CCRT; a transcript of part of one session; a CCRT scoresheet; a CCRT summary sheet; a discussion of the scoring of this transcript; and a summary of research on the CCRT method.

Steps in Scoring the CCRT

Follow the steps given below for scoring the CCRT and apply them to the transcript. Use as many pages as are needed of the CCRT scoresheet and the CCRT summary sheet. The particular transcript was chosen primarily for its value in providing practice in formulating the core theme rather than to illustrate the SE treatment principles. This transcript is the first 20 minutes of session 3 for a patient, Mr. B.N., who was at the time of the session a 21-year-old student in his last year of college. The 20-minute segment is adequate in this instance since it contains seven relationship episodes *(RE)*, a sufficient number for making a formulation. The *RE* have been marked off by an independent judge by a line in the left margin from the beginning to the end of the episode. At the beginning of the line the central object of the *RE* has been identified.

Six steps in arriving at the CCRT are summarized below. The first four steps are essential. Step 5 is optional; it provides more detailed information on the sequence of the interactions between the patient and the people described in the patient's *RE*. The sixth step provides information on the extent to which each component of the CCRT is part of the patient's experience of the relationship with the therapist and therefore can be considered a part of the patient's transference, as it is defined by Gill's method, [Gill and Hoffman 1982b].

Core Conflictual Relationship Theme

1. SCORING THE RE FOR THEME COMPONENTS

The judge reads and rereads the *RE* which have already been marked off on the transcript. In the course of reading each *RE* the judge underlines on the transcript each type of the three classes of theme components: the *W* (wishes, needs, and intentions), the *RO* (the responses from the object), and the *RS* (the responses from the self). The *RO* and *RS* are further divided into positive and negative consequences. An intensity rating can also be added after each component (mainly for research studies). At the end of this first step the judge transfers the scores on the transcript to the CCRT scoresheet along with the type of the component, such as the particular wish expressed.

2. MAKING A GENERAL CCRT FORMULATION

The judge reviews the scoresheet by inspecting it up and down across *RE* to find the formulations which apply to the most *RE*. This step is especially crucial for understanding of the *W*, while the *RO* and the *RS* tend not to require as much effort at abstracting the formulation.

Sometimes it is easy for the judge to abstract what is common across *RE*. At those times, for example, the general formulation of the *W* fits very closely with the directly expressed *W* of each *RE*. However, often during the process of reviewing the *W* across *RE* a general formulation on a more inferential level is necessary. It is important not to let the general formulation become more abstract than is necessary to fit a large number of the *RE*. It is this step 2 which especially requires the wet, gray software, that is, the cortex of a human judge, and is not likely soon to be supplanted by the dry, white hardware, that is, the computer.

3. REDOING THE SCORING IN STEP 1 FOR THE COMPONENTS OF THE GENERAL FORMULATION ACHIEVED IN STEP 2

The scoring of step 1 needs to be rechecked to be sure all of the components in the general formulation have been considered and scored if they are applicable. It is important to preserve the scoring from step 1 as separate from the revised scoring derived from applying the formulation achieved in step 2 so that it can be seen how often and how much change comes from the labor of step 2. Therefore use capital letters for the additions and alterations that come from step 2.

4. REMAKING THE GENERAL CCRT FORMULATION

All components are listed and tallied on the CCRT score sheet summary. The most frequent *W*, followed by the most frequent response from others, followed by the most frequent response from self, constitutes the CCRT.

5. RECORDING THE SEQUENCE OF THE INTERACTIONS (OPTIONAL)

A record of the sequence of the *W* and the responses of the patient and of others within each *RE* can add valuable information. It provides insight into each patient's typical relationship interaction sequences (as suggested by Dr. Ellen Berman, personal communication 1979). During the reading of the *RE*, the sequence of the appearance of the components of the theme can be noted by numbering them consecutively on the transcript (as in the example on p. 209 ff) and then transferring the sequence numbers to the CCRT scoresheet and the CCRT score sheet summary. Our experience with step 5 indicates that interactional sequences are highly stereotyped.

6. ESTIMATING THE PATIENT'S EXPERIENCE OF THE
COMPONENTS OF THE CCRT AND THEIR INVOLVEMENT IN THE
TRANSFERENCE

Since transference is defined as an experience of the patient, the judge is to categorize how each component of the CCRT is experienced.

Guides for Scoring Wishes, Needs, and Intentions Toward the Object: W

The judge reads the transcript with the *RE* located on it and scores two kinds of *W*. (1) *W* which are explicit, (2) *W* which are readily inferrable, *(W)*. If the *W* is not readily inferrable, no *W* score is provided for that *RE*.

EXAMPLE OF *W:*   Mr. B. N., *RE* 1)
"In the end of the fantasies I was—the position was reversed and I was stepping on *him* like that."

EXAMPLE OF *(W):*   Mr. B. N.
Sometimes the *(W)* becomes apparent only after reading the series of *RE*. The following is an example of a *(W)* which became apparent only as part of this general formulation step (step 2): *RE* 4: "I *really* don't want to get involved with her sexually" (i.e., wish to be sufficiently assertive to pull out of the relationship).

CHOOSING AMONG COMPETING WISH FORMULATIONS
Occasionally, the formulation of a general *W* presents a conceptualization problem. The judge may have to resolve an

ambiguity about which of two wishes is primary. The judge can usually make this decision on the basis of *frequency* of the various wishes, with the most frequent one being the primary one. Often the two competing wishes are closely related in the sense that they are the vortex of repeated conflict with each other. Beyond the frequency criteria, it has been noted that *sequence* tends to favor prior expression of the primary wish because of the narrative form. Furthermore, the primary wish tends also to be most consistent with the wish that is closest to what the patient wishes to affirm in relationships to people.

EXAMPLE: Mr. B. N. (the specimen case example at the end of this section).

His most frequent wish was, "I wish to assert myself in relation to pressures from other people, particularly their need to dominate." That wish to assert himself tends to compete with his wish to be close to people, to talk and share and be fed by them. The first wish would be called wish A and the second, wish B. Both should be scored, but relative frequency will identify wish A as the primary wish and wish B as the secondary, underlying wish.

EXAMPLE: Mr. T.M.

The judge was not sure which of these two wishes was primary, "I want to make a commitment to a person or to a job but it makes me feel too trapped." The other version of the wish was, "I want to avoid making a commitment to a person or to a job but I am under strong pressure to make such a commitment." The question for the judge was whether the wish to make a commitment or the wish to avoid making a commitment was the wish and which was the consequence of the wish. With Mr. T.M., there was some evidence that there was first an urge to make a commitment, then the feeling of being trapped, and then a wish to avoid making a commitment. Therefore, the wish to make a commitment is scored as the primary *W*.

EXAMPLE: Mr. S.B.

The patient frequently expressed strong wishes to hurt other people. An examination of the sequence showed that the wish to hurt other people was based on a prior unrequited wish, that is, to get a positive response from the other person. Therefore, the latter would be the primary wish and the wish to hurt others would be a subsidary wish.

An interesting principle about primary wishes is illustrated by these last two examples. There is a tendency for positive wishes to be primary. This trend sounds like a reflection of the judges' values and inclinations to affirm the basic goodness of human beings. Rather, it may be characteristic of the people who enter psychotherapy that they show a striving toward positive goals.

Guides for Scoring the Consequences from the Object or from the Self

These tend to be easier to score than the *W* since they are more directly expressed than the *W*. The *R* are of two kinds: responses from others *(RO)* and responses from self *(RS)*.

The designation "consequence" does not require of the judge that the responses be recognizable responses to the wish. It is sufficient for the judge to note all wishes and note all responses without having to connect the responses to the wishes.

POSITIVE AND NEGATIVE RESPONSES

Each type of response is further subdivided into mainly positive *(P)* or mainly negative *(N)* responses. "Negative" is defined as responses which mean to the patient that an interference with satisfaction of wishes has occurred or is expected to occur; "positive" refers to noninterference or expectation of noninterference with the satisfaction of wishes and/or a sense of mastery in being able to deal with the wishes.

EXPRESSED VERSUS CONSIDERED RESPONSES (TENTATIVE)

The subscripts $_{EXP}$ or $_{CON}$ can be applied to either *RO* or *RS*. An example of an *RS* $_{CON}$ is in Mr. B. M., page 210, "That irritated me." That was a considered response; the patient makes it clear that he did not express it to the object. On the other hand, the object did express to him domination, therefore, RO_{EXP}. The distinction between expressed and considered may be of value especially in studying the CCRT as a measure of change.

Scoring Intensity of Theme Components

Theme components vary in their intensity. A 1–5 scale may be sufficient for grading each one. (The sequence can also be noted as explained on p. 202).

EXAMPLE: Mr. B. N.

		Rating	Sequence
RE 1: I wish to assert myself: *(W)*		4	3
"He dominated by not	*RO*	4	1
letting me speak."			
"I was angry."	*RS*	5	2

Guides for Scoring the Patient's Experience of the Relationship

According to the psychoanalytic theory of psychotherapeutic change, patients should attain improved access to awareness of their experience in relationships, including the one with the therapist. A scoring of access to awareness should make possible a test of this thesis. The CCRT formulation of a session, since it often encompasses the interactions with the therapist, reflects the patient's experience of the relationship.

However, more precise scoring distinctions are needed. These should include the degree to which each component of the CCRT is experienced and the degree of corresponding awareness of the experience in the relationship with the therapist. Also needed is a distinction between awareness of the parallels between experience in the session versus outside the session, as put forward by Gill and Hoffman (1982a). In a strict sense, however, transference is only the experience of the relationship with the therapist in similar terms to the experience of the early parental relationships, not just in session versus outside of the session.

The distinctions of scoring below are mostly similar to those included in the Gill method of coding a patient's experience of the relationship with the therapist (Gill and Hoffman 1982a):

1. the degree to which the component is experienced in the relationship to the therapist (Gill's "*r*")
2. the degree to which the patient is aware of the experience in the relationship to the therapist (this is our label *ra*)

3. the degree to which the patient is aware of the parallel between the relationship to the therapist and outside relationships (Gill's "xr" and "rx").

4. the same as 3, except it is an inference by a judge that there is an implicit allusion to the patient's experience of the relationship in communications that are not manifestly about the relationship (Gill's *Jxr*).

Notations for Scoring the RE

RE = relationship episodes
RE_c = current RE
RE_p = past RE

Steps 1–4:

W = wish, need, or intention as directly stated by the patient

(W) = wish, need, or intention as inferred by the judge

RO = response from the "object" ("object" refers to the main person that the patient is interacting with in the RE)

RS = response from the self

N = negative (e.g., NRO = negative response from object)

P = positive

exp = expressed response to the object (e.g., NRS_{EXP} = negative response from self which is expressed)

con = considered but not expressed to the object

$\underline{1}, \underline{2}, \underline{3}, \underline{4},$ or $\underline{5}$ = a rating of the intensity of each theme component (W, RO, RS)

Step 5:

1, 2, 3, etc. = the sequence of each W, RO, and RS in each RE

Core Conflictual Relationship Theme

Step 6:

  r = experienced in the relationship with the therapist in the session

  ra = aware of being experienced in the relationship with the therapist in the session

  xr and rx = aware of the *parallel* between relationship with the therapist and outside relationships *(x)*

  Jxr and Jrx = inference by the judge of a *parallel* between relationship with the T and outside relationships, in communications that are not manifestly about the relationship

---

B.N. transcript (first 20 minutes of Session #3*)
_____

P₁: Hi!

T₁: How have you been?

RE #1

OBJECT: Guy (Roommate)

P₂: I've been feeling a little bit, uh, more alive lately, y'know, but I've had—I've had a lot of uh anxiety and nervousness connected with it. I haven't been sleeping too well, like uh, y'know, with just—with talking to people I—I feel better, things like that, uh. One thing that uh sorta just hit me, and I guess it's one of these delayed action things that that seems to happen to me quite a bit. There's this guy I was— lived with—lived with us for about a month during July and he's uh, I mean, we didn't get along too well, and uh whenever he got into a conversation or any-

---

*Annotate this transcript on its left margin following the directions given on pages 199–209. Then tally the scores on the CCRT Scoresheet (p. 221) and summarize on CCRT Scoresheet Summary (p. 222). Only then compare it with the scores of the four independent judges on the CCRT Scoresheet Summary (p. 223).

thing, y'know, he uh- he'd immediately try to dominate it and things like that. He did a lot of things that irritated me and at the time I guess I just, y'know, I repressed everything, and just sunk back. And lately I've been sort of brooding about it, and, y'know, I've been getting really worked up and pissed off over it, y'know, and then uh, uh, y'know, it's as I said, I said, it's a delayed action thing, I guess. It's like he was stepping on my toes a lot when I was there, you know, yet I didn't even have the guts to say "Ouch!" And that now that's—that's what all these fantasies were, y'know. It comes back and I—I put *him* down, and things like that.

T_2: What do you mean "fantasies?"

P_3: Uh, just thinking about it, and y'know, brooding on it, and uh waking, y'know, day dreams.

T_3: What are you doing to uh daydream.

P_4: Uh, y'know, it's usually in conversation, like uh, I remember one time there were—there were four of us and we were talking. And and I remember there there was a pause in the thing and he was doing all the talking and, uh, I had said something, and he turns to me and says, "Excuse me for interrupting" and then he, y'know, continues like that. It's this type of thing I was getting from him like the whole time he was there. And, uh, in the end of the fantasies I was, uh, the positions were reversed and I was stepping on *him* like that.

T_4: Um-huh.

P_5: (pause, 10 sec) It's uh, I guess I—y'know I can't really —that's a type of situation where I run into a person like that who- who, y'know, it's, it's one thing that I can't handle too well- I don't know how to cope with, uh, y'know, I usually have one of two types of reactions, either I, y'know, crawl back into a hole or, or I really snap out, y'know, bluntly, crudely and, uh, y'know I think there ought to be a better way to handle it but I'm not quite sure, y'know, how it's gonna work.

T_5:   By "snap out" you mean what?

P_6:   Uh, y'know, really, uh, come out with the hostilities that he arouses and things. He probab—in uh disproportionate to uh to what, what should grip, y'know, the reality of the situation, like uh, in, in one of the fantasies, uh, y'know, as I was reliving this thing where he uh—that, that incident I just described when he said, uh, "Excuse me for interrupting"—at the time I was dri—I was drinking a glass or water or something. And in this fantasy I threw the water in his face, or something like that (pause 10 sec) (clears throat) I think I—I tend to get abnormally worked up and you know frightened and—and angry at—at people who—who do things like this (pause, 10 sec).

T_6:   We were talking quite a bit about that last time.

RE #2
OBJECT: Policeman #2

P_7:   In fact I think, y'know, anybody who comes on as an —as an authority figure, y'know, tends to uh, y'know, when they're stepping on somebody it tends—it tends to really scare me. When I was—I was out in the park, Rittenhouse Square, the other day and uh some guy and his wife who, uh, I—who I had just met them, they were—they were sitting together on the bench and I guess the guy's wife had her leg draped over one of his legs, like this, and this cop comes up and he was talking like John Wayne and tells her to sit right. And well they stood up to him and, uh, you know, he finally carted them off and charged them with lewd and suggestive conduct or something like that, but while he was over there talking to them, I was just sitting, they were sitting on the bench and I was sitting on the wall behind them, and I—y'know, my heart started really beating fast and I got really anxious about it, y'know, I just sort of imagined what- what *I* would do in a situation like that, and I think what I would do was automatically (snaps fingers) obey the first thing he said (long pause, 35 sec).

T$_7$:   Could I bum a light off you, too?

RE #3

OBJECT: "Weird Guy"

P$_8$:   Oh, excuse me, sure (exhales). Another thing I've— I've been running into lately is like getting involved with people and getting friendly with people whom I—I guess tol—ultimately I really don't want to be friends with. Uh, there's this, uh, weird uh guy that's uh been hanging around campus for some years now. He's a big colored guy, six-four, three-ten or something like that. And I just met him and like uh, he comes around all the time and I really don't want him around and, uh, you know, it comes down to do I have a choice between being mean and being a hypocrite. Y'know, when I first met him I- he's a- y'know, I guess he's insanely insecure or something but he, uh, uh, goes out, y'know, goes out of his way to be outgoing and friendly and he's, he's witty, sometimes charming, like I can't—I can't, you know, I'm never gonna have any type of really, but, relationship with this guy because he doesn't get serious about anything and he's really a—well he's 29 years old and he's just bumming around and smoking pot, and things like that.

RE #4
OBJECT: Girl with the "clap"

But like, uh, I-I have this girl, uh, I know uh, been cooking dinners for me lately and like, y'know, there's a—I really don't want to get involved with her sexually because I heard some bad rumors about her like she has the clap or something like that which—and uh—I, y'know, I just can't talk to her that well either although, y'know, maybe if I saw her once a month I could, y'know, carry on a piece of conversation or something like that but I get too close to these people that I can't really get close to and I keep doing things like this, not too close but too uh involved, I guess.

T_8: Well, what do you think you're seeking when you're —

P_9: Well, y'know, I guess, uh, I'm just sort of a (pause) a hungry to have people around that I can talk to, things like that.

T_9: Why do you need them for?

P_{10}: I don't know, it's uh—usually pretty hard, hard for me to just, to just be alone. And uh well this has been sort of a pattern that developed in the, y'know, past couple of years, y'know, just to be alone or—or to uh, to really get into uh something that does interest me, and I apparently haven't found out uh, y'know, what I can do and what I like to do, really like to do yet.

T_{10}: What happens when you're alone?

P_{11}: Uh, usually I get, I get really bored, I can't, I can't, I don't know what to do with myself.

T_{11}: And then what happens?

P_{12}: Usually I sort of, uh, just lay back and accept it, lethargically (pause 5 sec) I, y'know, I think I probably tend to withdraw, y'know, but uh I, y'know, I don't think I uh, uh, y'know, y'know given a specific situation where I'm alone and I don't necessarily go out and then look for it, y'know, other people or anybody to, to talk to uh, usually.

T_{12}: Well, you you seem to dislike being alone, and I'm just wondering what's bad about it.

P_{13}: The same thing uh that y'know that happens to me when I'm I'm alone and as when I get into a, a situation where there's a group, group of people talking and— I'm not really saying that much. I feel very — uncomfortable and like I'm, y'know, I'm not really sure I exist for, for other people, for some reason. Y'know, maybe it's because I'm not really too aware of uh myself. (pause)

T_{13}: There is I gather a feeling of quite a lot of anxiety in being alone.

P_{14}: Yeah. (pause) Like, like I used to be able to uh to read a lot, and do things like that but like, uh, now I find that, y'know, when I'm reading or something like I feel like I should be out doing something else, like, like relating to people. Y'know, I have this—y'know, it's, it's uh not quite, I guess, a—well, maybe it is a compulsion to uh, y'know go out there and and uh, y'know, because I seem to think that's where it's really, really at, or something.

T_{14}: Yeah but you seem to have carried it to the point that

you know that you don't really count for anything
unless you do relate to people.

P$_{15}$:   Uh, yeah.

T$_{15}$:   Or something. (pause) And you can't seem to be
satisfied just being alone—

P$_{16}$:   Yeah—

T$_{16}$:   —yourself—

RE #5

OBJECT: Therapist

P$_{17}$:   Yeah, I feel like I, I have to go out and prove myself
or something like that. I have to go out and come
across to people and and impress them. (long pause,
35 sec) I think what's uh happening to me right now
in here is uh typical of a situation when I start feeling
better, when I start feeling more, y'know, aware,
more alive, more interested in things. And that's at
uh, y'know I get to a point where I, want to, I want
to, I want to go back- I want to close up again.

T$_{18}$:   Are you feeling that way now?

P$_{17}$:   Yeah, well, y'know, I think, you know, that's why I'm
I'm probably having trouble talking and discussing
things.

T$_{18}$:   I'm not sure you're having that much trouble talking
unless you interpret the silences we've had—

P$_{19}$:   Well—

T$_{19}$:   —as voids that need to be filled.

P$_{20}$:   Yeah, yeah, I tend to do that a lot.

T$_{20}$:   Do you think that's true necessarily?—

P$_{21}$:   Uh- I guess, I guess it really—

T$_{21}$:   —do we have to fill every space with something?

P$_{22}$:   No. I guess I should play it cooler, be able to be a little cooler about it, I mean, rather than getting worked up about it, y'know, silence, or something like that. (pause) I don't know what- what I just said about, y'know, withdrawing, is really true right now.

RE #6
OBJECT: Dr. T. (Former Therapist)

But like that's what's—that's what's happened in the past. Whenever I get so I am feeling more alive and more stronger, uh, I—I tend to have—have tendencies to retreat, uh, and, uh, like uh, the sessions that I had with Dr. T. there were a couple of them where, you know, when I was feeling pretty good where I didn't—I didn't really—they weren't really that productive, or I didn't really talk about that much or—or anything like that. And like uh, I guess uh, I didn't see him for about a- about a month, toward the end of uh of last—last Fall semester, I guess, uh, December, and then part of November I didn't see him at all. And uh, I was feeling better then, y'know, stronger and more alive than I had in a long time (long pause, 15 sec).

T_{22}:   Dr. T.'s come up in our conversations a few times. Do you think you miss him?

P_{23}:   Um (pause 5 sec) well not really—um (long pause, 10 sec) I mean right now I don't really feel that I do.

T_{23}:   Do you think you have some feelings about his leaving?

P_{24}:   Uh, I don't know.

T_{24}:   You had—you had worked with him for a year.

P_{25}:   I hadn't, you know, I guess I do, but uh, like, like the last session was really, was really pretty good and y'know it was sort of a fitting in, I think. (pause 5 sec) I didn't—I didn't feel really, you'know, at least immediately I didn't feel that uh, anxious about it, or —or up—upset about it at all. You know, right now I really can't see that there's, you know, there's much, much to that.

T$_{25}$: Well, I was just wondering.

P$_{26}$: (10 sec pause) You know, I think I took the, y'know, the change y'know the—sanely, eh sanely as I, as I've taken any, any change (35 sec pause). I've been wondering about uh, I guess, uh the future a little bit more now. And like uh next semester I'm going to be carrying a heavy load, and a lot of things. I'm going to be taking six courses and uh, one of the courses I want to take is like uh a dry course and it's, it's more hours than a normal course, and it's also a lot of work outside of class, and then I'm gonna have to have a job, and I hope to have a—a cycle, which is gonna take some—some of my time. And it's probably as— as heavy a load as I've I've ever carried in a semester. It's m—it's heavier. And—and I think like my sophomore year, the second semester of my sophomore year when I was working in this hospital as an orderly, I sort of loaded myself up with a lot of things to do, and I just—toward the end of it, uh, I, y'know, I quit, y'know, I got—I got into all these things and then all y'know I suddenly, suddenly withdrew, and, uh, sort of, uh, wondering about, y'know, since something like that is going to happen in the next semester.

T$_{26}$: The question is why are you taking on so many things, if you find them hard to carry.

P$_{27}$: Well, I think I haven't, y'know, I'm—I'm capable of it, y'know, I have the stuff in me to do it, uh, I have to take six courses I—and also—

T$_{27}$:   How about the job? Why are you—

P$_{28}$:   Well, I'm gonna need the job. I need the money. Like the cycle is sort of, I guess I don't really need that, like I want to—

T$_{28}$:   You mean you need the job because you're going to spend the money on the cycle—

P$_{29}$:   Probably— (laughing)

T$_{29}$:   —is that correct?

P$_{30}$:   Well, uh—well, it's uh—I'm gonna need the job partly because of that but like the money I was going to use to buy the cycle is not money that I really needed. It was money that I was going to keep in the bank and let it collect interest and then having that backing me up, uh—. I guess I want to—I want to fill up my life a little bit more. I've been sort of a- the boredom has been really getting to me, this summer. And I just want to get into these, these things, like uh, uh the cycle. It's something I'm going to have to get into. I'm going to have to learn—learn how to take care of it, and things like that, because I know nothing, mechanically. And, uh, right now, y'know, I sort of uh pleasurably anticipate uh learning something about things like this. And uh, y'know, the same thing with that drawing course, I'd like to get into, fool around with something like that. It's, uh, the course, I guess, the teacher I hear is pretty good. Like he doesn't really care about your uh technical ability to render so much as he cares about getting you to learn how to *see*, y'know, to be aware of uh space, architectural space and perspective, and things like that. And I'm uh kind of excited over—over getting, y'know, getting into something like that (15 sec pause).

T$_{30}$: Well, what, what I'm wondering is, whether you're going to have enough time to do as well in all these things as you would like to do.

P$_{31}$: I don't know.

T$_{31}$: Whether you're going to be so busy you won't be able to do any of them well and then you'll drop it all. Well that's what you're wondering, I guess.

P$_{32}$: Yeah. But I was also thinking of—of—of something else sort of that uh y'know, I'm—I'm almost, you know, anxious about getting into something that I really like, and lot of these things appeal to me (15 sec pause). Because I think I'm gonna have enough time because I'm really not that uh concerned at all about uh grades.

T$_{32}$: Well, um, what?

P$_{33}$: Uh, uh, one semester, uh, one thing I don't think I'm gonna do badly, and uh, another thing is that, uh, I'm not—I don't feel any particular pressure to do excellently, y'know, even though I think I might have some capabilities to do pretty well because like one semester is not going to make, uh, that much difference in my *cum*, which is uh, just a little bit above average right now (15 sec pause). I mean like if I got *C*'s in everything it wouldn't particularly bother me, y'know, depending on how much work I have to do in uh—(20 sec pause). I guess it's sort of basically right now I sorta feel like I'm on the verge of something, y'know, uh that I'm anticipating uh getting into things that are gonna be uh rewarding, exciting (10 sec pause).

219

RE #7

OBJECT: Mother

> I uh called home last night and I talked to my mother about uh, y'know, the money for the cycle. Originally when I first thought of the idea of getting it, y'know, I thought of doing it, was sort of behind their back and just waiting till the money came then uh, y'know, buying it, sort of as a shock and a surprise to them but y'know as, as I said, I think I said once before I think I have a genuine interest in uh in getting a motorcycle on—and it's, you know, so I called and I —and I didn't run into any problems at all. She said that she thought I was old enough to make a decision like this for myself etcetera, etcetera. And uh, there's also sort of a technical matter that I want to get the bike before school starts, so I had to ask to sen—for the money to be sent cause I wouldn't have gotten it till later (15 sec pause). I think I still have sort of an ulterior motive in buying a cycle, y'know, and-and-and this is uh—I don't know if it's totally ulterior, but like it's along lines of impressing people. (end of 20 min.)

Discussion of the Scoring of Mr. B.N. by Four Independent Judges

After the reader has scored the transcript, the scoring should be compared with the sample of four judges' scoring in the CCRT summary (p. 223). The four judges were not highly experienced in the use of the CCRT method. They had had only a few hours of previous experience with the method,

Core Conflictual Relationship Theme

RE # Object Page #	Wish, Need, Intention	Response from Object	Response from Self

Patient # _____	CCRT Scoresheet	Date of Scoring _____
Session # _____	Summary	Name of Scorer _____
Number of RE _____		

Wish, Need, Intention	RATERS				Response from Object	RATERS				Response from Self	RATERS			
					NEGATIVE					NEGATIVE				
					POSITIVE					POSITIVE				

Core Conflictual Relationship Theme

Patient # __B.N.__	CCRT Scoresheet Summary *	Date of Scoring _____
Session # ___3___		Name of Scorer _____
Number of RE ___7___		

Wish, Need, Intention — RATERS

Wish, Need, Intention	V	C	J	K
A. To assert myself	7	6	7	7
1. To reject others, not to go along with others	2	1	3	2
2. To impress others	1	2	2	1
3. To feel strong, alive, interested	1	3	0	0
4. To be able to do what I want, not be dominated	3	0	0	1
5. To express myself, communicate more effectively	0	0	1	1
6. To avoid withdrawing	0	0	1	1
7. To prove myself sexually	0	2	0	0
8. To be independent	0	1	0	0
9. To feel good about myself without withdrawing	0	0	1	1
B. To be close with another	0	1	1	0

Response from Object — RATERS

Response from Object	V	C	K	J
NEGATIVE				
a. Domination	2	1	3	2
b. Intrusion (those I don't want to be close with are frequently around)	0	0	2	1
c. Rejection	0	1	0	0
d. Therapist unable to treat me	0	0	1	0
e. Disapproval of decisions	0	0	0	1
POSITIVE				
a. Gives approval, does not reject; respects decisions	1	0	1	1
b. Does not dominate	0	1	0	0
c. Reassurance from others (that I'm OK)	0	0	1	0
d. Does not interfere, or intrude	0	0	1	0
e. Gives help	1	0	0	0

Response from Self — RATERS

Response from Self	V	C	K	J
NEGATIVE				
a. Withdraw	3	3	4	3
b. Passivity; go along with others	2	3	3	3
c. Anger, being "mean"	4	0	3	2
d. Frightened, anxious	2	2	1	2
e. Feeling repressed	1	1	1	0
f. Fantasize about dominating others	1	1	0	0
g. Act in a hypocritical way	1	0	0	1
h. Conceal actions	1	0	1	0
i. Lose autonomy	0	1	0	0
j. Loss of sense of self in attempt to be close	0	1	0	0
k. Act in a way which doesn't correspond to feelings	1	0	0	0
l. Feel need to impress others	1	0	0	0
m. Seek approval	1	0	0	0
n. Unable to communicate effectively	0	0	1	0
o. Afraid of being alone	0	0	0	1
POSITIVE				
a. Express my own wishes, opinions	0	0	1	3
b. Increased self-esteem; feel alive, strong, interested	0	1	1	0
c. Not to withdraw	0	0	1	1
d. Control my own decisions	0	1	0	0
e. Feel comfortable about interactions with therapist	0	0	0	1

*Tabulation of the types of CCRT components identified in the transcript by four independent raters.

mostly from reading the guide (Luborsky 1983). For all judges this case was the first one they scored. Two of them were experienced clinicians, one was a psychiatrist, the other a psychologist, both of whom had had a year of experience treating patients in psychotherapy under the supervision of the author and using this manual as a guide. Two were undergraduate psychology majors. It is of interest to see in the summary that despite these differences in background and clinical experience the tally of their scores showed a fair amount of agreement. The following were the general findings:

1. The CCRT can be read almost directly from the tallies in the CCRT scoresheet summary. For example, for judge V the general wish identified as "to assert myself" was evident in 7 out of 7 of the *RE*. The other judges showed similarly high proportions of the same general wish. For this patient the CCRT is as follows: *W:* "I wish to assert myself" (mainly in the sense of not going along with the demands of others); *RO:* "They express domination"; *RS:* (but) "I withdraw and become passive as well as frightened and anxious."

2. Interjudge agreement is more evident for the *W* than for the *RO* and *RS*. The principle appears to be that agreement is greater on those components which are more frequent. From this small sample of judges it appears that clinical experience is not the essential condition for agreement of judgments. In fact agreement for this set of judges is high, even though for all four they are less experienced than the four who rated the same case in the Levine and Luborsky study (1981).

3. Negative *RO* and *RS* are more common than positive ones for this patient. In fact this is a strong trend for all patients who have been scored with the CCRT.

Summary of CCRT Research

The CCRT was developed as a measure of a pervasive relationship pattern. Because that relationship pattern appears in relationships with the therapist just as it does in outside-of-treatment relationships, it is justified to call the CCRT a measure of transference. The theory of psychoanalytically oriented psychotherapy postulates that it is the reexperiencing and working through of this recurrent relationship pattern which is the central change agent. This variable is, therefore, the main one which should be measured during and at the end of psychoanalytically oriented psychotherapies to determine the degree to which therapy has been focused on this theme and the degree to which changes have taken place in it. It would be of great value to determine whether other different psychotherapies produce similar changes in the CCRT but the field lacks any well-developed measures of this variable. That was the recurrent theme at the NIMH Coolfont, West Virginia Conference on Psychotherapy Research in October 1982. The CCRT method was one of the first quantitative measures of the transference pattern that were based on psychotherapy sessions and in which the pattern was expressed as a formulation. A brief summary of the research on the CCRT follows; more detail can be found in Luborsky (1977), Levine and Luborsky (1981), and Luborsky, *A Guide to the CCRT*, in preparation.

RELIABILITY

Agreement of judges on the types of CCRT components has been examined in one study (Levine and Luborsky 1981). Good agreement was found between 16 graduate psychology student judges who scored the CCRT individually, and the composite of four research judges' scoring. Furthermore, the agreement of the judges has also been shown by the method of "mismatched cases", that is, agreement is greater for judging types of components from the Mr. B.N. case itself than for those pairs which included the purposely mismatched types from two other cases.

CONSISTENCY OF THE CCRT OVER TIME

The types of CCRT components appear to have considerable consistency over time, even from early to late in long-term treatment. This finding emerges from the comparison of the early CCRT with the late CCRT for the 15 patients in the Penn Psychotherapy Project (Luborsky 1977). Of these patients, the less improved appeared to have greater consistency over time than the more improved. Furthermore, the wish component tended to be more consistent over time than the response component.

Several studies are in progress on the degree of consistency of the CCRT over time e.g. Gerin et al. in preparation. These studies should help develop the CCRT method as a measure of change in psychoanalytically oriented psychotherapy.

The next example is a sample of the use of the CCRT for comparing the early and late CCRT. A more quantitative comparison can be obtained by inserting the frequencies based on the scoring.

EXAMPLE: Mr. L.

The initial CCRT wish formulation was: "I wish to express myself and to be heard and to be able to be competitive with and better than other men." The consequences were: "I will not be able to tolerate this wish because it will make me feel guilty (response from self) and they will not be able to tolerate it because of their fragility and depression" (response from others).

At the time of the termination, the CCRT wishes were much the same. The consequences, however, had changed somewhat: the patient was more comfortable about expressing his interests, describing his superior abilities (response from self), and recognizing that his doing this could be acceptable and be tolerated by other men or women (response from others).

CONSISTENCY OF THE CCRT FOR RELATIONSHIPS TO PARENTS VERSUS RELATIONSHIPS TO THE THERAPIST

This comparison has special interest because it could provide a basis for the usual assumption that transference is involved in the CCRT measure. If it is found that the CCRT pattern for the parents in the past is like that for the therapist, such results would be consistent with the concept of transference.

CONSISTENCY OF CCRT BASED ON PSYCHOTHERAPY SESSIONS VERSUS BASED ON NARRATIVES REQUESTED BY AN INTERVIEWER OUTSIDE OF PSYCHOTHERAPY

This study is in progress on six patients from the Penn Psychotherapy Project with the data available from both sources (van Ravenswaay, Luborsky and Childress, in preparation). The outside-of-treatment narratives are obtained through a standardized format called the Relationship Anecdotes Paradigms Test(RAP test) (Luborsky, typescript 1978). The major question of this research is whether the relationship patterns established during SE psychoanalytically oriented psychotherapy are special to psychotherapy or are more broadly representative of the patient's outside-of-treatment relationship patterns. So far, the latter alternative is the impression provided by the first results.

COMPARISONS OF THE CCRT METHOD WITH OTHER MEASURES
OF THE TRANSFERENCE PATTERN

Since the advent of the CCRT method(Luborsky 1977), other apparently similar quantitative measures of transference patterns have been developed or have been recognized to be similar. One of the best known of these allied methods is the Gill and Hoffman method (1982a) for assessing the patient's experience of the relationship with the therapist (Gill 1982; Gill and Hoffman 1982b). The evidence that the CCRT is the theme which is typically involved in transference phenomena is provided by the presence of the same CCRT in *RE* about the therapist as in outside of treatment relationships. Further exploration of this issue may be provided by inclusion of the scoring categories of the patient's experience of the relationship with the therapist (similar to Gill's categories). Another well-known system is the unconscious plan method of the Mount Zion psychotherapy research group (Weiss and Sampson 1984). Comparisons of the CCRT with these methods are being planned.

Appendix 5

Rating Scales for Supportive-Expressive Psychoanalytically Oriented Psychotherapy

The scales provided in this appendix are intended to further one of the main purposes of the manual, namely, to determine the degree to which SE psychotherapy was performed by each psychotherapist. All of them are generally related to parts of the manual and help to describe the nature of each treatment.

These scales listed below for rating psychotherapy sessions are given in sequence:

Rating scales for the main distinctive characteristics of SE psychotherapy

Rating scales for supportiveness

    Therapists' ways of facilitating the helping alliance, type 1

    Therapists' ways of facilitating the helping alliance, type 2

Rating scales for understanding

Rating scales for the quality of the therapist's response
Rating scale for therapist skill
Rating scale for degree of help provided

The first set of scales consists of three distinctive aspects of SE and a summary scale for rating the degree to which the sample is consistent with the characteristics of SE.

The next set of scales are for rating supportiveness; they include 12 therapist facilitative behavior scales for estimating what the therapist does which might facilitate or impede the development of a helping alliance. The first seven are those which might facilitate type 1 helping alliance and the next five are those which might facilitate type 2 helping alliance.

The next set of scales are to evaluate the therapist's understanding of the patient. They relate to principles of understanding 1, 3, and 5.

The next set consists of eight scales on the therapist's responding in terms of the aim to achieve understanding by expressive means. Some of these scales emerged from a discussion with Dr. Helmut Thomä on the need to enlarge the number of scales dealing with the therapist's adequacy of responding to the expressions in the treatment of the transference pattern. These therapist response scales are to be rated for the session as a whole. They can, in addition, be used to evaluate a sample of the individual responses of the therapist.

In addition to the above scales for rating the psychotherapy sessions, another scale is presented for related studies: This is a rating scale for the patient's experience of a helping alliance (to be filled out by the patient).

The following has a brief résumé of SE psychotherapy as described in this manual to help orient the judge who would be rating samples of the therapy.

An Introduction to Rating Supportive–Expressive Psychotherapy

Supportive–expressive psychotherapy is a patient-centered therapy in the sense that the therapist listens, understands, and responds on the basis of what the patient is saying rather than on the basis of responses prepared in advance. The therapist and patient take a problem-solving approach to the meaning of the symptoms and the related interpersonal problems.

*SUPPORTIVE TECHNIQUES

The therapist must decide initially and as the treatment progresses whether the treatment can rely primarily on expressive techniques or whether additional attention to support is needed. For some patients the therapist gives enough support to allow the patient to tolerate as much expressiveness as possible. The most central ways of providing support and strengthening the alliance include: conveying a sense of sympathetic understanding; assisting the patient to maintain vital defenses and activities which bolster areas of competence; demonstrating a realistically hopeful attitude; recognizing the patient's ability to use the basic tools of the treatment and do what the therapist does; and engaging with the patient in a joint search for understanding.

*EXPRESSIVE TECHNIQUES

The therapist follows the flow of the patient's thoughts in order to discern the meaning of the symptoms and the associated relationship problems expressed in the core conflictual

*The asterisk in the margin besides a technique in the SE manual means that it is considered most central.

relationship theme (CCRT). During each session the therapist is (1) listening, (2) making a formulation, (3) responding to what the patient is saying, and then (4) listening further.

Rating Scales

Rater's Name _____   Session # _____
                              (or Tape #)

Rating Scales for the Main Distinctive Qualities of SE

There are four scales, three for the main distinctive qualities of SE and a fourth for an overall rating of the degree to which the therapy fits the characteristics of SE psychotherapy. These four scales were successfully used to distinguish samples of supportive–expressive, cognitive–behavioral, and drug counseling (Luborsky, Woody, McLellan, O'Brien, and Rosenzweig 1982; Woody, Luborsky, McLellan, O'Brien, Beck, Blaine, Herman, and Hole 1983)

1. The degree to which the treatment is focussed on giving support: by developing a helping alliance, bolstering areas of competence, and by encouragement and support of healthy defenses and activities

1	2	3	4	5
None	Some	Moderate	Much	Very Much

2. The degree to which the treatment is focused on facilitating self-expression as part of the search for understanding

1	2	3	4	5
None	Some	Moderate	Much	Very Much

3. The degree to which the treatment is focused on the understanding of the relationship with the therapist and its basis in the transference

1	2	3	4	5
None	Some	Moderate	Much	Very Much

4. The degree to which the treatment fits the manual's specifications of supportive–expressive psychoanalytically oriented psychotherapy (a summary scale)

1	2	3	4	5
None	Some	Moderate	Much	Very Much

Rating Scales for Supportiveness

Therapist's Ways of Facilitating the Helping Alliance: Type 1

1. Conveying through words and manner support for the patient's wish to achieve the goals

1	2	3	4	5
None	Some	Moderate	Much	Very Much

2. Conveying a sense of understanding and acceptance

1	2	3	4	5
None	Some	Moderate	Much	Very Much

3. Developing a liking for the patient

1	2	3	4	5
None	Some	Moderate	Much	Very Much

4. Assisting the patient to maintain vital defenses and to maintain activities which bolster morale, areas of competence, and general level of functioning

1	2	3	4	5
None	Some	Moderate	Much	Very Much

5. Communicating a realistically hopeful attitude that the treatment goals are likely to be achieved (or, at least, a willingness to continue to try to help to achieve them)

1	2	3	4	5
None	Some	Moderate	Much	Very Much

6. Giving recognition, on appropriate occasions, that the patient has made some progress toward the patient's goals

1	2	3	4	5
None	Some	Moderate	Much	Very Much

7. Encouraging some patients on some occasions to express themselves, especially in areas in which they wish to be helped

1	2	3	4	5
None	Some	Moderate	Much	Very Much

Therapist's Ways of Facilitating the Helping Alliance: Type 2

1. Encouraging a "we bond"

1	2	3	4	5
None	Some	Moderate	Much	Very Much

2. Conveying respect for the patient

1	2	3	4	5
None	Some	Moderate	Much	Very Much

3. Conveying recognition of the patient's growing sense of being able to do what the therapist does in using the basic tools of the treatment

1	2	3	4	5
None	Some	Moderate	Much	Very Much

4. Referring to experiences that the patient and therapist have been through together

1	2	3	4	5
None	Some	Moderate	Much	Very Much

5. Engaging in a joint search for understanding

1	2	3	4	5
None	Some	Moderate	Much	Very Much

Rating Scales for Understanding

Principle 1. Understanding the patient's main symptoms, main sources of psychic pain, and changes in these, in terms of their associated theme

1	2	3	4	5
None	Some	Moderate	Much	Very Much

Principle 4. Attending to each sphere of the relationship triad (1) current relationships in treatment, (2) current relationships out of treatment, and (3) past relationships

1	2	3	4	5
None	Some	Moderate	Much	Very Much

Principle 6. Seeing the symptoms as problem-solution or coping attempts

1	2	3	4	5
None	Some	Moderate	Much	Very Much

Principle 7. Attending to the patient's perception of the therapist's behavior

1	2	3	4	5
None	Some	Moderate	Much	Very Much

Rating Scales for the Therapist's Adequacy of Responding in Terms of Expressive Aims

Principle 1. The degree to which the therapist's response deals effectively with a facet of the main relationship problem—the core conflictual relationship problem (CCRT)

1	2	3	4	5
None	Some	Moderate	Much	Very Much

Principle 1A. The degree to which the therapist also relates the CCRT to one of the symptoms.

1	2	3	4	5
None	Some	Moderate	Much	Very Much

Principle 1B. The degree to which the therapist's responses are directed to the most emotion-laden or pressing part of the patient's transference issue

1	2	3	4	5
None	Some	Moderate	Much	Very Much

Principle 2. The degree to which the therapist's responses recurrently recognize and deal adequately with a facet of CCRT so as to facilitate the working through

1	2	3	4	5
None	Some	Moderate	Much	Very Much

Principle 3. The degree to which the therapist recognizes the patients' need to test the relationship in transference terms and passes the test

1	2	3	4	5
None	Some	Moderate	Much	Very Much

Principle 7. The degree to which the therapist's responses pass the matching-of-messages test, that is, they match the message of the patient in an adequate and effective way

a. State in a sentence the essence of the patient's main message in the session: _____

b. State in a sentence the essence of the therapist's responses in the session: _____

c. Rate the degree to which the therapist's message is an adequate and effective response to the patient's message.

1	2	3	4	5
None (Miss the main point)	Some	Moderate	Much	Very Much (Hit on the main point)

Principle 8. The degree to which the therapist's responses are directed to the part of the transference issue which is closest to the patient's awareness

1	2	3	4	5
None	Some	Moderate	Much	Very Much

Principle 9. The degree to which the therapist presents responses in a form which is appropriately simple and uncomplex so as to be maximally understandable to the patient

1	2	3	4	5
None— Inappropriately overcomplex	Some	Moderately understand- able	Much	Very Much Appropriately simple and understand- able

Principle 12. The degree to which the therapist's responses are free of countertransference distortions

1	2	3	4	5
None Not free of them	Some	Moderately free of them	Much	Very Much Free of them

Rating Scale for the Therapist's Skill

The degree to which the therapist is conducting this treatment skillfully and competently

1	2	3	4	5
Poorly	Mediocre	Fairly Well	Excellently	Outstanding

Rating Scale for Degree of Help Provided

The degree to which the patient believes the therapist is providing help. For example: "I was pleased with the new understanding you gave me in the last session" or, "I am really happy with the help I'm getting from you."

1	2	3	4	5
Very little or none	Some	Moderate amount	Much	Very much

Rating Scales

Rating Scale for the Patient's Experience of the Helping Alliance (to be filled out by the patient as described in Alexander and Luborsky, 1984):

Name _____
Date _____

The Helping Relationship Questionnaire

Below are listed a variety of ways that one person may feel or behave in relation to another person. Please consider each statement with reference to your present relationship with your therapist.

Mark each statement according to how strongly you feel that it is true, or not true, in this relationship. *Please mark every one.* Write in +3, +2, +1 or −1, −2, −3, to stand for the following answers:

+3. Yes, I strongly feel that it is true

+2. Yes, I feel it is true

+1. Yes, I feel that it is probably true, or more true than untrue

−1. No, I feel that it is probably untrue, or more untrue than true

−2. No, I feel it is not true

−3. No, I strongly feel that it is not true

_____ 1. I believe that my therapist is helping me.
_____ 2. I believe that the treatment is helping me.
_____ 3. I have obtained some new understanding.
_____ 4. I have been feeling better recently.
_____ 5. I can already see that I will eventually work out the problems I came to treatment for.
_____ 6. I feel I can depend upon the therapist.
_____ 7. I feel the therapist understands me.
_____ 8. I feel the therapist wants me to achieve my goals.

———— 9. I feel I am working together with the therapist in a joint effort.

————10. I believe we have similar ideas about the nature of my problems.

————11. I feel now that I can understand myself and deal with myself on my own (that is, even if the therapist and I were no longer meeting for treatment appointments).

Kinds Of Change:

I feel improved in the following ways: _____

_____

_____

I feel worse in the following ways: _____

_____

_____

Estimate of Improvement so Far:

1	2	3	4	5
Not at all	Slightly	Moderately	Much	Very Much

References

Alexander, F., and French, T. 1946. *Psychoanalytic therapy: Principles and applications.* New York: Ronald Press.

Alexander, L., and Luborsky, L. 1984. Research on the helping alliance. *In the psychotherapeutic process: A research handbook,* L. Greenberg, and W. Pinsof. eds. New York: The Guilford Press.

Alexander, L.; Luborsky, L.; Auerbach, A.; Cohen, M.; Ratner; H.; and Schreiber, P. 1982. The effect of the match between patient and therapist: Findings from the re-pairing study. Paper delivered at the Society for Psychotherapy Research Meeting.

American Psychiatric Association, Commission on Psychiatric Therapies (T. Karasu, Chair). 1982. Manual for Psychiatric Treatments. Washington, D.C. Typescript.

American Psychological Association. 1980. Psychotherapy Research Supported, *APA Monitor,* 1.

Atthowe, J. 1973. Behavior innovation and persistence. *American Psychologist* 28: 34–41.

Auerbach, A. 1963. An application of Strupp's method of content analysis of psychotherapy. *Psychiatry* 26: 137–48.

Auerbach, A. H., and Luborsky, L. 1968. Accuracy of judgments of psychotherapy and the nature of the "good hour." In *Research in psychotherapy,* vol. 3, eds. J. Shlien, H. F. Hunt, J.P. Matarazzo and C. Savage, 155–68. Washington, D.C.: American Psychological Association.

Balint, M.; Ornstein, P.; and Balint, E. 1972. *Focal psychotherapy.* London: Tavistock Publications.

Beck, A. T., and Emery, G. D. 1977. *Individual treatment manual for cognitive behavioral psychotherapy for drug abuse.* Copyright 1977 (1st ed. 11/1/77). Typescript.

Beck, A. T.; Rush, A.; Shaw, B; and Emery, G. 1979. Cognitive Therapy of depression: A treatment manual. (Copyright by A.T. Beck, 1978). Typescript.

Bergin, A., and Lambert, M. 1978. The evaluation of therapeutic outcomes. In *Handbook of psychotherapy and behavioral change: An Empirical Analysis,* eds. S. Garfield and A. Bergin, New York: Wiley.

Bergmann, M., and Hartman, F. (eds.). 1977. *The evolution of psychoanalytic technique.* New York: Basic Books.

Berlinski, D. 1978. Catastrophe theory and its applications: A critical review *Behavioral Science* (September), *23,* 402–416.

Berzins, J. 1977. Patient–therapist matching, In *Effective psychotherapy,* eds. A. Gurman and A. Razin, Oxford, U.K.: Pergamon Press, 222–251.

Bibring, E. 1954. Psychoanalysis and the dynamic psychotherapies. *Journal of the American Psychoanalytic Association* 2: 745–70.

Blanton, S. 1971. *Diary of my analysis with Sigmund Freud.* New York: Hawthorne.

Brady, J. P. 1970. Behavior therapy. In *Modern trends in psychological medicine,* ed. J. H. Price, 256–76. London: Butterworth.

Brenman, M. 1952. On teasing and being teased and the problem of "moral masochism." *Psychoanalytic Study of the Child,* 7: 264–85. New York: International Universities Press.

Brunink, S., and Schroeder, H. 1979. Verbal therapeutic behavior of expert psychoanalytically oriented, Gestalt, and behavior therapists. *Journal of Consulting and Clinical Psychology,* 47: 567–74.

Burstein, A. 1976. Psychotherapy for the poor. In *Successful psychotherapy,* ed. J. L. Claghorn, 189–96. New York: Brunner/ Mazel.

Butcher, J., and Koss, M. 1978. Research on brief and crisis-oriented therapies. In *Handbook of psychotherapy and behavior change,* eds., S. Garfield and A. Bergin. New York: Wiley.

Butler, J. M., and Rice, L. N. 1963. Adience, self-actualization and

References

drive theory. In *Concepts of personality,* eds. J. Wepman and R. Heine, Chicago: Aldine.

DeRubeis, R.; Hollon, S.; Evans, M.; and Bemis, K. 1982. Can psychotherapies for depression be discriminated? A systematic investigation of cognitive therapy and interpersonal therapy. *Journal of Consulting and Clinical Psychology,* 50: 744–56.

DiMascio, A.; Klerman, G.; Weissman, M.; Prusoff, B.; Neu, C.; and Moore, P. 1979. An ethically justifiable and methodological appropriate control group for psychotherapy research in acute depression. Typescript.

Docherty, J.; Marder, S.; Van Kammen, D.; and Siris S. 1977. Psychotherapy and pharmacotherapy: conceptual issues. *American Journal of Psychiatry, 134:* 529–533.

Edelson, M. 1963. *Termination of intensive psychotherapy.* Springfield, Illinois: Charles C Thomas.

Ekstein, R. 1969. The learning process: From learning for love to love of learning. In *From Learning for Love to Love of Learning,* Ekstein, R. and Motto, R. eds. 95–98. New York: Brunner/Mazel.

———. 1980. Robert Waelder's criteria of interpretation(1939) revisited. *Journal of the Philadelphia Association for Psychoanalysis* 7: 113–128.

Ekstein, R., and Wallerstein, R. 1958. *The teaching and learning of psychotherapy.* New York: Basic Books.

Feldman, F. 1968. Results of psychoanalysis in clinic case assignments. *Journal of the American Psychoanalytic Association* 16: 274–300.

Feldman, F.; Lorr, M.; and Russell, S. 1958. A mental hygiene clinic case survey. *Journal of Clinical Psychology* 14:245–50.

Fenichel, O. 1930. Statisticher bericht über die therapeutische tatigkeit, 1920–1930. In *Zehn jahr Berliner psychoanalytisches institut,* ed. 13–19. Wien: Internationale Psychoanalytischer Verlag,

———. 1941. Problems of psychoanalytic technique. *The Psychoanalytic Quarterly* 7.

References

Ferenczi, S. [1920] 1950. *Further contribution to the theory and technique of psychoanalysis.* London: Hogarth Press.

Fiske, D. W.; Cartwright, D. S.; and Kirtner, W.L. 1964. Are psychotherapeutic changes predictable? *Journal of Abnormal and Social Psychology* 69:418-26.

Frank, J. 1968. The role of hope in psychotherapy. *International Journal of Psychiatry* 5: 383-95.

French, T., and Wheeler, D. 1963. Hope and the repudiation of hope in psychoanalytic therapy. *International Journal of Psychoanalysis* 44: 304-16.

Freud, S. [1911] 1958. The handling of dream-interpretation in psychoanalysis. In *The standard edition,* vol. 12, ed. J. Strachey, 89-96. London: Hogarth Press and the Institute of Psychoanalysis.

—————. [1912]. 1958. The dynamics of transference. In *The standard edition,* vol. 12, ed. J. Strachey, 97-108. London: Hogarth Press and the Institute of Psychoanalysis. (a)

—————. [1912] 1958. Recommendations to physicians practicing psycho-analysis. In *The standard edition,* vol. 12, ed. J. Strachey, 109-120. London: Hogarth Press and the Institute of Psychoanalysis. (b)

—————. [1913] 1958. On beginning the treatment (further recommendations on the technique of psychoanalysis.) In *The standard edition,* vol. 12, ed. J. Strachey, 121-44. London: Hogarth Press and the Institute of Psychoanalysis. (a)

—————. [1913] 1958. The claims of psychoanalysis to the interest of the non-psychological sciences. In *The standard edition,* vol. 13, ed. J. Strachey, 165-92. London: Hogarth Press and the Institute of Psychoanalysis. (b)

—————. [1914] 1958. Remembering, repeating and working-through. Further recommendations on the technique of psychoanalysis.) In *The standard edition,* vol. 12, ed. J. Strachey, 147-56. London: Hogarth Press and the Institute of Psychoanalysis.

References

————. [1915] 1957. The unconscious. In *The Standard Edition*, vol. ed. J. Strachey, 166–204. London: The Hogarth Press and the Institute of Psychoanalysis. (a)

————. [1915] 1958. Observations on transference-love: Further recommendations on the technique of psychoanalysis. In *The standard* edition, vol. 12, ed. J. Strachey, 157–71. London: Hogarth Press and the Institute of Psychoanalysis. (b)

————. [1926] 1959. Inhibitions, symptoms, and anxiety. In *The Standard Edition*, vol. 20, ed. J. Strachey, . London: Hogarth Press and The Institute for Psychoanalysis. 87–174.

————. [1932] 1964. The dissection of the psychical personality. In *The Standard Edition*, vol. 22, ed. J. Strachey, 57–80. London: Hogarth Press and the Institute of Psychoanalysis.

————. [1937]1964. Analysis terminable and interminable. In J. Strachey(ed.). *The standard edition*, vol.23, ed. J. Strachey, 216–54. London: Hogarth Press and The Institute for Psychoanalysis.

GAP. 1975. Pharmacotherapy and psychotherapy: paradoxes, problems and progress. Report 93 NY: GAP.

Gerin, P, Baguet, J. and Sali, H. Measuring change in psychotherapy by the Core Conflictual Relationship theme method, in preparation.

Gill, M. M. 1951. Ego psychology and psychotherapy. *Psychoanalytic Quarterly* 20: 60–71.

————. 1954. Psychoanalysis and exploratory psychoanalysis. *Journal of the American Psychoanalytic Association*, 2:771–90.

————. 1979. The analysis of the transference. *Journal American Psychoanalytic Association* (Supplement): 263–88.

————. 1982. Analysis of transference. *Theory and technique*, vol. 1 of *Psychological issues*, Monograph 53. New York: International Universities Press.

Gill, M. M., and Hoffman, I. Z. 1982. A method for studying the analysis of aspects of the patient's experience of the relationship in psychoanalysis and psychotherapy. *Journal of the American Psychoanalytic Association* 30: 137–67. (a).

————. 1982. Analysis of transference. *Studies of nine audio-recorded psychoanalytic sessions,* Vol. 2 of *Psychological issues,* Monograph 54. New York: International Universities Press. (b)

Glover, E. 1955. *The technique of psycho-analysis.* New York. International Universities Press.

Goldstein, A. P., and Simonson, N. R. 1971. Social psychological approaches to psychotherapy research. In *Handbook of psychotherapy and behavior change,* eds. A. E. Bergin and S. L. Garfield. New York: Wiley.

Greenblatt, M. 1959. Discussion of papers by Saslow and Matarazzo and Lacey. In eds. E. Rubinstein and M. Parloff, 209–20. "Research in Psychotherapy," Washington, D.C., American Psychological Association.

Greenson, R. 1965. The working alliance and transference neurosis. *Psychoanalytic Quarterly* 34: 158–81.

————. 1967. *The technique and practice of psychoanalysis.* Vol. 1. New York: International Universities Press.

Greenspan, S. 1981. Psychopathology and adaptation in infancy and early childhood: Principles of clinical diagnosis and preventive intervention. *Clinical Infant Reports,* No. 1, New York: International Universities Press. (a)

Greenspan, S., and Polk, W. 1980. A developmental approach to the assessment of adult personality functioning and psychopathology. In *The course of life: Psychoanalytic contributions toward understanding personality development,* vol. 3, eds. S. Greenspan, and G. Pollock Washington, D.C.: Government Printing Office.

Greenspan, S., and Sharfstein, S. 1981. The efficacy of psychotherapy: Asking the right questions. *Archives of General Psychiatry* 38: 1213–19.

Grinker, R., and Spiegel, J. 1944. Brief psychotherapy in war neuroses. *Psychosomatic Medicine* 6: 123–31.

————. 1945. *Men under stress* Philadelphia: Blakiston.

Henry, W.; Sims, J.; and Spray, S. 1973. *Public and private lives of psychotherapists,* 272. San Francisco: Josey-Bass.

References

Herink, R. (ed.). 1980. *The psychotherapy handbook: The A to Z guide to more than 250 different therapies in use today.* New York: New American Library (Meridian).

Hoehn-Saric, R.; Frank, J.; Imber, S.; Nash, E.; Stone, A.; and Battle, C. 1964. Systematic preparation of patients for psychotherapy: I. Effects on therapy behavior and outcome. *Journal of Psychiatric Research* 2: 267–81.

Hollender, M. 1965. *The practice of psychoanalytic psychotherapy.* New York: Grune & Stratton.

Holt, R., and Luborsky, L. 1958. *Personality patterns of psychiatrists,* Vol. 1. New York: Basic Books.

Holzman, P. 1965. Process in the supervision of psychotherapy. *Bulletin Menninger Clinic* 29: 125–30.

Horowitz, L. M.; Sampson, H.; Sigelman, E.; Wolfson, A.; and Weiss, J. 1975. On the identification of warded-off mental contents. *Journal of Abnormal Psychology* 84: 545–58.

Horowitz, M. 1979. *States of mind: Analysis of change in psychotherapy.* New York: Plenum.

Horowitz, M.; Marmar, C.; and Wilner, N. 1979. Analysis of patient states and state transitions. *Journal of Nervous and Mental Disease* 167: 91–99.

Janis, I. (ed.). 1982. *Counseling on personal decisions: Theory and research on short-term helping relationships.* New Haven Conn.: Yale University Press.

———. 1983. Short term counseling: Guidelines based on recent research. New Haven: Yale University Press.

Karasu, T. B. 1981. From Freudian psychoanalysis to experiential psychotherapies: An essay on recent trends. *Academy Forum* (Summer) 25: 13–31.

Kernberg, O. 1975. *Borderline conditions and pathological narcissism.* New York: Jason Aronson.

Kernberg, O.; Burstein, E.; Coyne, L.; Applebaum, A.; Horowitz, L.; and Voth, H. 1972. Psychotherapy and psychoanalysis: Final report of the Menninger Foundation's psychotherapy research project. *Bulletin of the Menninger Clinic* 36: 1–275.

Klein, G. 1970. *Perception, motives and personality.* New York: Knopf.

Klerman, G., and Neu, C. 1976. A manual for interpersonal treatment of depression. Typescript.

Klerman, G.; Rounsaville, B.; Chevron, E.; Neu, C.; and Weissman, M. 1979. Manual for short-term interpersonal psychotherapy (IPT) for depression. Yale University, New Haven, Conn. 4th draft. Mimeo.

Kohut, H. 1977. *The restoration of the self.* New York: International Universities Press.

Levine, F., and Luborsky, L. 1981. The core conflictual relationship theme method—A demonstration of reliable clinical inferences by the method of mismatched cases. In *Object and self: A developmental approach,* eds. S. Tuttman, C. Kaye, and M. Zimmerman, 501–26. New York: International Universities Press.

Lindemann, E. 1944. Symptomatology and management of acute grief. *American Journal of Psychiatry* 101: 141–48.

Lipton, S. Review of Blanton (1971). 1973. *Bulletin of the Philadelphia Association for Psychoanalysis* 23: 236–37.

———. 1979. An addendum to: The advantages of Freud's techniques as shown in his analysis of the Rat Man. *International J. Psychoanalysis* 60, 215–216.

Luborsky, L. Repeated intra-individual measurements (P-Technique) in understanding symptom structure and psychotherapeutic change. In O. H. Mowrer (ed.) *Psychotherapy: theory & research.* New York: Ronald Press, 1953 (Chapter 14).

———. 1962. The patient's personality and psychotherapeutic change. In *Research in psychotherapy,* vol. II, eds. H. Strupp and L. Luborsky. 115–33. Washington, D.C.: American Psychological Association.

———. 1973. The task of the psychotherapist—A socratic dialogue between the therapist and the supervisor in psychoanalytically oriented psychotherapy. Typescript.

———. 1967. Momentary forgetting during psychotherapy and psychoanalysis: A theory and research method. In *Motives and*

References

thought: Psychoanalytic essays in honor of David Rapaport. ed. R. R. Holt 177–217. New York: International Universities Press.

———. 1969. Research cannot yet influence clinical practice. (An evaluation of Strupp and Bergin's *Some empirical and conceptual bases for coordinated research in psychotherapy: Critical review of issues, trends and evidence.*) *International Journal of Psychiatry* 7:135–40.

———. 1970. New directions in research on neurotic and psychosomatic symptoms. *American Scientist* 58: 661–68.

———. 1976. Helping alliances in psychotherapy: The groundwork for a study of their relationship to its outcome. In *Successful psychotherapy,* ed. J. L. Claghorn, 92–116. New York: Brunner/Mazel. (a)

———. 1976. *A general manual for supportive–expressive psychoanalytically oriented psychotherapy.* Typescript. (Copyright 1976). (b)

———. 1977. Measuring a pervasive psychic structure in psychotherapy: The core conflictual relationship theme. In *Communicative structures and psychic structures.* eds. N. Freedman and S. Grand, 367–95. New York: Plenum.

———. 1978. Relationship narratives as a basis for inference about transference. Typescript.

———. 1978. The relationship anecdotes paradigms test (RAP test): A TAT-like method using actual narratives. Typescript.

———. 1983. A guide to the core conflictual relationship theme method: Directions for scoring and a review of related research. Typescript.

Luborsky, L., and Auerbach, A. H. 1969. The symptom–context method: Quantitative studies of symptom formation in psychotherapy. *Journal of the American Psychoanalytic Association* 17: 68–99.

———. 1979. *Manual for nonscheduled minimal treatment,* (Adapted from A. DiMascio, G. Klerman, M. Weissman B. Prusoff, C. Neu, and P. Moore. [1978], Typescript.

Luborsky, L.; Chandler, M.; Auerbach, A. H.; Cohen, J.; and

References

Bachrach, H. M. 1971. Factors influencing the outcome of psychotherapy: A review of quantitative research. *Psychological Bulletin* 75: 145–85.

Luborsky, L.; Crits-Christoph, P.; Alexander, L.; Margolis, M.; and Cohen; M. 1983. Two helping alliance methods for predicting outcomes of psychotherapy: A counting signs vs. a global rating method. *Journal of Nervous Mental Disorder. 171:* 480–492.

Luborsky, L.; Docherty, J.; Todd, T.; Knapp, P.; Mirsky, A.; and Gottschalk, L. 1975. A context analysis of psychological states prior to petit mal seizures. *Journal of Nervous and Mental Disease* 160:282–98.

Luborsky, L. and De Rubeis, R. 1984. The use of psychotherapy manuals: A small revolution in psychotherapy research style. *Clinicial Psychology Review* 4.

Luborsky, L. B.; Fabian, M.; Hall, B. H.; Ticho, E.; and Ticho, G. 1958. Treatment variables. *Bulletin of the Menninger Clinic* 22: 126–47.

Luborsky, L.; Graff, H.; Pulver, S.; and Curtis, H. 1973. A clinical–quantitative examination of consensus on the concept of transference. *Archives of General Psychiatry* 29: 69–75.

Luborsky, L., and McLellan, A. T. 1981. Optimal matching of patients with types of psychotherapy: What is known and some designs for knowing more. In *Matching patient needs and treatment methods for alcohol and drug abuse,* eds. E. Gottheil, A. T. McLellan, K. Druley 51–71. Chicago: Charles Thomas.

Luborsky, L.; McLellan, A. T.; Woody, G.; O'Brien, C.; and Auerbach, A. In preparation. Therapists' success and its determinants.

Luborsky, L.; Mintz, J.; Auerbach, A.; Christoph, P.; Bachrach, H.; Todd, T.; Johnson, M.; Cohen, M.; and O'Brien, C. P. 1980. Predicting the outcomes of psychotherapy—Findings of the Penn psychotherapy project. *Archives of General Psychiatry* 37: 471–81.

Luborsky, L.; Mintz, J.; Auerbach, A.; and Crits-Christoph, P with the collaboration of Bachrach, H., and Cohen, M. In preparation.

References

Psychotherapy: Who will benefit and how?—Factors influencing the outcomes of psychotherapy.

Luborsky, L.; Sackeim, H.; and Christoph, P. 1979. The state conducive to momentary forgetting. In *Functional disorders of memory.* eds. J. Kihlstrom and F. Evans, 325–53. Hillside, N.J.: Lawrence Erlbaum.

Luborsky, L.; Singer, B.; Hartke, J.; Crits-Christoph, P.; and Cohen, M. 1983. Which concepts of depression fit the context of Mr. Q's shifts? In eds. L. Rice and L. Greenberg. *Patterns of Change: Intensive analysis of psychotherapy process,* New York: Guilford Press.

Luborsky, L., and Schimek, J. 1964. Psychoanalytic theories of therapeutic and developmental change: Implications for assessment. In *Personality change,* eds. P. Worchel and D. Byrne, 73–99. New York: Wiley.

Luborsky, L.; Singer, B.; and Luborsky, L. 1975. Comparative studies of psychotherapies: Is it true that "Everybody has won and all must have prizes"? *Archives of General Psychiatry* 32: 995–1008.

Luborsky, L.; Woody, G.; Hole, A.; and Velleco, A. In preparation. *Treatment manual for supportive–expressive psychoanalytically oriented psychotherapy—Special adaptation for treatment of drug dependence,* copyright 1977. In *Psychological treatment manuals and their effectiveness for drug abuse patients.* eds. G. Woody, L. Luborsky, and T. McLellan.

Luborsky, L.; Woody, G. E.; McLellan, A. T.; O'Brien, C. P.; and Rosenzweig, J. 1982. Can independent judges recognize different psychotherapies? An experience with manual-guided therapies. *Journal of Consulting and Clinical Psychology* 30: 49–62.

Malan, D. H. 1963. *A study of brief psychotherapy.* London: Tavistock Publications.

———. 1976. *Toward the validation of a dynamic psychotherapy.* New York: Plenum.

Mann, J. 1973. *Time-limited psychotherapy.* Cambridge, Mass.: Harvard University Press.

References

Mayman, M. 1978. Trauma, stimulus barrier, ego boundaries and self-preservation: Ego psychology in *Beyond the pleasure principle.* In *The human mind revisited: Essays in honor of Karl A. Menninger,* ed. S. Smith, 141–58. New York: International Universities Press.

McLellan, A. T.; Luborsky, L.; Woody, G.; O'Brien, C.; and Druley, K. 1983. Predicting response to alcohol and drug treatments: Role of psychiatric severity. *Archives of General Psychiatry.* 40: 620–25.

McLellan, A. T.; Luborsky, L.; O'Brien, C.; Druley, K.; and Woody, G. 1983. Increased effectiveness of substance abuse treatment—A prospective study of patient-treatment "matching" *J. Nervous and Mental Disease,* 171: 597–603

Menninger, K. 1942. *Love against hate.* New York: Harcourt, Brace.

————. with Mayman, M. and Pruyser, P. 1963. *The vital balance:* The Life Process in Mental Health and Illness. New York: Viking Press.

Menninger, K., and Holzman, P. S. 1973. *The theory of psychoanalytic techniques.* 2nd ed. New York: Basic Books.

Minuchin, S. 1974. *Families and family therapy.* Cambridge, Mass.: Harvard University Press.

Morgan, R.; Luborsky, L.; Crits-Christoph, P.; Curtis, H.; and Solomon, J. 1982. Predicting the outcomes of psychotherapy by the Penn helping alliance rating method. *Archives of General Psychiatry* 39: 397–402.

Nash, E.; Hoehn-Saric, R.; Battle, C.; Stone, A.; Imber, S.; and Frank, J. 1965. Systematic preparation of patients for short-term psychotherapy. II. Relation of characteristics of patient, therapist and the psychotherapeutic process. *Journal of Nervous and Mental Disease* 140:374–83.

Neu, C.; Prusoff, B.; and Klerman, G. 1978. Measuring the interventions used in the short-term interpersonal psychotherapy of depression. *American Journal of Orthopsychiatry,* 48: 629–36.

Orne, M., and Wender, P. 1968. Anticipatory socialization for psychotherapy: Method and rationale. *American Journal of Psychiatry* 124:88–98, 1209–11.

Parloff, M. B. 1979. Can psychotherapy research guide the policy-maker? A little knowledge may be a dangerous thing. *American Psychologist* 34:296–306.

Pfeffer, A. Z. 1959. A procedure for evaluating the results of psychoanalysis: A preliminary report. *Journal American Psychoanalytic Association* 7:418–44.

Ramzy, I. 1974. How the mind of the psychoanalyst works: An essay on psychoanalytic inference. *International Journal Psychoanalysis,* 55:543–50.

Ramzy, I., and Shevrin, H. 1976. The nature of the inference process: A critical review of the literature. *International Journal of Psychoanalysis* 57:151–59.

Rapaport, D.; Gill, M. M.; and Schafer, R. 1968. *Diagnostic psychological testing.* rev.ed., R.R. Holt, ed. New York: International Universities Press.

Rank, O. 1936. *Will therapy?* New York: Knopf.

Redl, F. 1966. *When we deal with children.* New York: Free Press.

Rogers, C. 1957a. The necessary and sufficient conditions of therapeutic personality change. *Journal of Consulting Psychology* 21:-95–103.

Rogers, C. 1957b. Training individuals to engage in the therapeutic process. In C. R. Struther (ed.) *Psychology and Mental Health,* Washington D.C.: American Psychological Association pp. 76–92.

Rounsaville, B.; Weissman, M.; and Prusoff, B. 1981. Psychotherapy with depressed outpatients: Patient and process variables as predictors of outcome. *British Journal of Psychiatry* 138:-67–74.

Rounsaville, B.; Glazer, W.; Wilbur, C.; Weissman, M.; and Kleber, H. 1983. Short-term interpersonal psychotherapy in Methadone-maintained Opiate Addicts. *Archives of General Psychiatry* 40:629–36.

Sampson, H. 1976. A critique of certain traditional concepts in the psychoanalytic theory of therapy. *Bulletin of the Menninger Clinic* 40:255–62.

Schafer, R. 1958. On the psychoanalytic study of retest results. *Journal of Projective Techniques* 22:102–109.

Schlesinger, H. 1969 Diagnosis and prescription for psychotherapy. *Bulletin Menninger Clinic,* 33:269–78.

Schlesinger, H. 1977. The responsibility of the psychoanalyst for analytic and therapeutic change. In *The transactions of the Topeka psychoanalytic society.* recorder, A. Appelbaum. *Bulletin of the Menninger Clinic* 41:202–206.

Schmale, A. H. 1958. Relationship of separation and depression to disease. *Psychosomatic Medicine* 20:259–77.

Sifneos, P. W. 1972. *Short-term psychotherapy and emotional crisis.* Cambridge, Mass.: Harvard University Press.

Silberschatz, G. 1977. The effects of the analyst's neutrality on the patient's feelings and behavior in the psychoanalytic situation. Ph.D. diss. New York University.

Singer, B., and Luborsky, L. 1977. Countertransference: A comparison of what is known from the clinical vs quantitative research. In *The therapist's contribution to effective psychotherapy: An empirical assessment,* eds. A. Gurman and A. Razin. New York: Pergamon.

Sloane, R. B.; Staples, F. R.; Cristol, A. H.; Yorkson, N. J.; and Whipple, K. 1975. *Psychotherapy vs. behavior therapy.* London and Cambridge, Mass.: Harvard University Press.

Smith, M.; Glass, G.; and Miller, T. 1980. *The benefits of psychotherapy* Baltimore: Johns Hopkins Press.

Spence, D. P. 1973. Tracing a thought stream by computer. In *Psychoanalysis and contemporary science,* vol. 2, ed. B. B. Rubinstein. New York: Macmillan.

Spence, D. P., and Lugo, M. 1972. The role of verbal cues in clinical listening. In *Psychoanalysis and contemporary science,* vol. 1, eds. R. Holt and E. Peterfreund, 109–131. New York: Macmillan.

Stone, L. 1951. Psychoanalysis and brief psychotherapy. *Psychoanalytic Quarterly* 20:215–36.

References

――――. 1961. *The psychoanalytic situation*. New York: International Universities Press.

Stone, P. J.; Dunphy, D. C.; Smith, M. S.; and Ogilvie, D. M. 1966. *The general inquirer*. Cambridge, Mass.: MIT Press.

Strupp, H. 1958. The performance of psychoanalytic and client-centered therapists in an initial interview. *Journal of Consulting Psychology*. 22: 265–74.

Strupp, H., and Binder J. 1982. Time-limited dynamic psychotherapy(TLDP): A treatment manual. Typescript. (Copyright 1982).

Van Ravenswaay, P, Luborsky, L & Childress, A. Consistency of the transference in vs out of psychotherapy. Paper given at Society for Psychotherapy Research, July, 1983.

Waelder, R. (1939) 1976. Criteria of interpretation In *Psychoanalysis: Observation, theory, application-selected papers by Robert Waelder*. S. Gutman (Ed.) New York: International Universities Press.

Wallerstein, R. 1984. *Forty-Two lives in treatment*. New York: Guilford Press.

Wallerstein, R., and Robbins, L. 1956. Concepts. In *The psychotherapy research project of the Menninger Foundation*, R. Wallerstein, L. Robbins, H. Sargent, and L. Luborsky. *Bulletin Menninger Clinic* 20:239–62.

Wallerstein, R.; Robbins, L.; Sargent, H.; and Luborsky, L. 1956. The psychotherapy research project of the Menninger Foundation. Rationale, method and sample use. *Bulletin of the Menninger Clinic* 20:221–80.

Waskow, I. E.; Hadley, S.; Parloff, M.; and Autry, J. 1979. *Psychotherapy of depression*. Collaborative Research Program. Unpublished interim research proposal. National Institute of Mental Health.

Weiss, J. 1971. The emergence of new themes: A contribution to the psycho-analytic theory of therapy. *International Journal of Psychoanalysis*, 52: 459–67.

Weiss, J. and Sampson, H. 1984. *The psychotherapeutic process*. Guilford Press: New York.

Weissman, M. 1979. The psychological treatment of depression—Evidence for the efficacy of psychotherapy alone in comparison with, and in combination with pharmacotherapy. *Archives of General Psychiatry* 36: 1261–69.

Witaker, C and Malone, T. 1981. *The roots of psychotherapy* New York: Brunner/Mazel.

Witkin, H.; Lewis; H. B.; and Weil, E. 1968. Affective reactions and patient–therapist interaction among more differentiated and less differentiated patients early in therapy. *Journal of Nervous and Mental Disease* 146:1930–2008.

Wolberg, L. R. 1967. *The technique of psychotherapy.* 2nd ed. New York: Grune & Stratton.

Wolpe, J. 1969. *The practice of behavior therapy.* New York: Pergamon.

Woody, G. E.; Luborsky, L.; and McLellan, T. In Preparation. *Psychological treatment manuals for drug abuse patients and evidence for their effectiveness.*

Woody, G. E.; Stockdale, D.; and Hargrove, E. 1977. *A manual for drug counseling.* Copyright, 1977. Typescript.

Woody, G.; McLellan, A. T.; Luborsky, L.; and O'Brien, C. P. 1981. Psychotherapy for opiate addiction:Some preliminary results. *Annals of the New York Academy of Sciences,* 362:91–100.

Woody, G.; Luborsky, L.; McLellan, A. T.; O'Brien, C. P.; Beck, A.; Blaine, J.; Herman, I.; and Hole, A. 1983. Psychotherapy for Opiate Addicts—Does it Help? *Arch. Gen. Psychiat, 40,* 639–45.

Zetzel, E. 1958. The therapeutic alliance in analysis of hysteria. In *The capacity for emotional growth,* chap. 11, ed. E. Zetzel. 182–96. Hogarth Press:London.

Index

Index

Control function, 19–20
Core conflictual relationship theme (CCRT), 160; CCRT method in formulation of, 107–10, 133; clinical methods in formulation of, 98–107, 133; early recognition of, 94; focusing on one facet of, 121–23; focusing responses to, 69; increased mastery and, 20–21, 151–52; in matching-of-messages test, 133, 134; and patient's perception of therapist's behavior, 115–17; recurrent recognition of, 123–25, 179; returning to listening and, 141; after termination, 20, 151–52; in theory of psychotherapeutic change, 16–21; therapist's staying with, 131–32; in three relationship spheres, 110–13, 127; two classes of components in, 19–20; wish-consequence form of, 107, 110–11, 114–15, 132, 203–6; working through and, 124
Core conflictual relationship theme (CCRT) method, *xxii*, 6, 13, 107–10, 133, 199–228; development of, *xxi*, 225; discussion of judges' sample scoring, 220–25; as focus of responses, 121; guides for scoring consequences from object or self, 205–6; guides for scoring patient's experience of session, 207–8; guides for scoring wishes toward object, 203–5; as measure of transference, 225; methods similar to, 108, 228; notations for RE measurement, 208–9; sample session transcript, 209–20; scoresheets, 221–23; scoring intensity of theme components, 206; six steps for scoring, 200–203; summary of research on, 225–28; ther-

apist's inadequate response to transference and, 128
Countertherapeutic response, 140
Countertransference, 83, 137–39
Coyne, L., 55
Cristol, A. H., 34, 55
Crits-Cristoph, P., *xxii*, 26–27, 29, 54, 79, 95, 138, 169
Curtis, H., *xxii*, 79, 108

Danger situations, 109–10
DC, *see* Drug counseling
Defenses, need for strengthening of, 25, 73, 77, 83
Depression: precipitous, 95; understood by its context, 95
Depression Collaborative study (NIMH), 33
DeRubeis, R., 5, 38, 40
Developmental level, psychotherapeutic change and, 21
Diagnostic evaluation, pretreatment: and choice of SE-TL, 160–61, 185; and choice of treatment procedures, 161; and need for supportive techniques, 73; neuropsychological, 76; physical, 173–74; sample report of, 185–91
Diazepam, 170–71
Dislike of patient, 83
DiMascio, A., 32
Docherty, J., 95, 172
Drug abuse, psychiatric severity as predictor in, 55
Drug counseling (DC): degree of supportiveness in, 72; manual-based, research findings on, 35–38; manuals for, 31–32
Druley, K., *xxii*, 53

Index

Gill, Merton M., *xx*, 9, 23, 25, 73, 83, 83*n*, 108, 112, 117, 128, 200, 207–8, 228

Glass, G., *xv*, 4, 31, 84–85, 170

Glazer, W., 37

Glover, E., 121

Goals, *see* Treatment goals

Goldstein, A. P., 51

Gottschalk, L., 95

Graff, H., 108

Greenblatt, M., 138

Greenson, R., 9, 25, 79

Greenspan, S., 21

Grinker, R., 8

Group supervision, 44, 46, 49, 76–77

Group treatment in SE, 166–69

Guide to the CCRT, A (Luborsky), 225

131–32; *see also* Supportive relationship

Henry, W., 3

Herink, R., *xvi*

Herman, I., 232

Hoehn-Saric, R., 51

Hoffman, I. Z., 108, 117, 128, 200, 207–8, 228

Hole, A., 232

Hollender, M., 9

Hollon, S., 38

Holt, Robert R., *xx*, 43

Holzman, Philip S., *xv-xviii, xx, xxi,* 8, 15, 110, 113

Hopefulness about treatment goals, 83–86

Horowitz, L., 55

Horowitz, M., 97, 108, 119

Hospitalized patients, 7

Hadley, S., 33

Hall, B. H., 9

Hargrove, E., 35

Hartke, J., 95

Hartman, F., 9

Helping alliance: achievement of, as curative factor, 21, 24–25, 28; counting signs rating method (HA_{CS}) for, 79–82; definition of, 6, 79; global rating method (HA_R) for, 79–80; positive vs. negative transference and, 24–25, 81; predictive value of, *xxii*, 79–81; rating scale for patient's experience of, 230, 239–40; type 1 methods of facilitating patient's experience of, 81–87, 233–34; type 2 methods of facilitating patient's experience of, 87–89, 234–35; therapist's staying with CCRT and,

Id, 20; derivatives of, 19

Imber, S., 51

Inference: principles of, 118–19; type of psychotherapy and degree of, 33–34

Insight, *see* Self-understanding

Intention, *see* Wish, need, or intention

Intentionality, patient's, 6

"Internal markers of goal achievement," 63

Internalization, 26–28

Interpersonal psychotherapy (IPT): Depression Collaborative study on, 33; manual-based, research findings on, 34–35, 37–39; manuals for, 32

Interpretation, *xx;* CCRT and, 6; limiting complexity of, 136; sup-

Index

Index

Singer, B., *xv*, 4, 31, 54, 84–85, 95, 137, 139, 144
Siris, S., 172
Sloane, R. B., 34, 35, 37, 38, 55, 82
Smith, M., *xv*, 4, 31, 84–85, 170
Socialization, *see* Preliminary socialization interview
Solomon, J., *xxii*, 79
Speaking vs. silence, 162–63; encouragement of, 87; treatment rules on, 64
Spence, D. P., 94, 141
Spiegel, J., 8
Spray, S., 3
Staples, F. R., 34, 55
States of mind: intolerable, and goal setting, 63, 78; shifts in, 97–98, 119
"Stereotype plates," 18
Stockdale, D., 35
Stomach pains, 95
Stone, A., 51
Stone, L., 8, 9, 15
Strupp, H., 32, 33
Supervision, *see* Training and supervision
Supportive-expressive psychoanalytically oriented psychotherapy (SE), *xxi–xxii;* analogies for, *see* Analogies; change in, *see* Change, psychotherapeutic; classical psychoanalysis and, 4, 7–10, 12, 15, 64; combined with psychopharmacologic agents, 7, 169–73; definition of, *xix–xx*, 3, 12; essential features of, 4, 7–12; expansion of treatment group in, 166–69; face-to-face position in, 12; as focal therapy, 160; frequency of sessions in, 12; manual–based, research findings on, 35–38; manuals for, 32; Menninger

Foundation and, *xix–xxi*, 4, 7, 9, 43–44; patient suitability for, 54; post-classical psychoanalysis and, 4, 6, 8; prevalence of use of, 3; psychotherapy research and, 3–4, 7, 34–38; range of patients, 7–9, 54; rating of, *see* Rating scales; sequence of steps in, 13–14; time structure of, 6–8, 12, 64, 66, 143–45, *and see* Time-limited psychotherapy (SE-TL) *and* Time open-ended psychotherapy (SE-TO); training in, *see* Training and supervision; *see also* Beginning treatment; Expressive techniques; Supportive relationship; Termination
Supportive relationship, 6, 13, 62, 71–89, 231; in classical psychoanalysis, 11, 25, 71–72, 82; deciding on kind of extra support needed, 74–75; deciding on need for strengthening of, 25, 73–78; definition of, *xx*, 11, 71; in emphasis of treatment, 7, 9, 10, 73–74; and expressive techniques, 71, 73–75; facilitation of, 11, 21, 25, 81–89, 233–35; as inherent to psychotherapy, 25, 71–73; patient's experience as definitive of, 24–25, 72; psychotherapy research on, 72; response principles of early sessions and, 69; rating scales for, 81–82, 229, 230, 233–35; transference and, 11, 24–25, 81; *see also* Helping alliance
"Sympathetic understanding," 25, 72, 82
Symptoms: definition of, 94–95; focusing of response and, 121; and formulation of CCRT, 98–107; listening and location of, 94; and

Index

mination, 143, 152–54; marking treatment milestones and, 146–47; measurement of, *see* Core conflictual relationship theme (CCRT) method; patient's need to test relationship with therapist, 125–26; resistance and, 23; and supportive relationship, 11, 24–25, 81; working through and, 124

Transference potentials, 18, 23, 17–18

Treatment arrangements, 64–67; checklist for, 183–84

Treatment goals, 13; hopefulness about, 83–86; improvement in symptoms and, 17; monitoring progress by, 62–63; reviewing, 78; SE-TL vs. SE-TO and, 160; setting of, 61–63; supportive relationship and, 11; therapist's expression of support for, 82; and transference potentials, 18; *see also* Termination

Treatment-patient matching, *see* Patient-treatment matching

Treatment principles: listed, 9–12; *see also specific techniques*

Treatment structure: facilitation of helping alliance by, 25; steps in, 13–14; supportive relationship and, 11; *see also* Length of treatment; Termination

Tree-in-dense-forest analogy, 178–79

Trust: establishment of, 13, 67–68; *see also* Supportive relationship

"Unconscious plan," 108, 126, 228

Understanding, 93–119; adequacy of, and timing of response, 136–37; and administration of medications, 172; CCRT method for formulation of relationship theme, 107–10; clinical formulation of relationship theme, 98–107; definition of, 24, 91; joint search for, 89; patient's, *see* Self-understanding; of patient's perception of therapist, 115–17; principles of inference and, 118–19; rating scales for, 229, 230, 235–36; reviewing and, 113–14; of shifts in "states of mind," 97–98; of symptoms in context of relationship, 94–97; of symptoms as problem-solution attempts, 114–15; therapist's communication of, 82, *and see* Responding; of triad of relationship spheres, 110–13

Universität Ulm, Department of Psychotherapy of, *xxiii*

Van Kammen, D., 172
van Ravenswaay, P., 227
Voth, H., 55

Waelder, Robert, 177
Wallerstein, Robert, *xx*, 9, 25, 44, 48, 55, 90
Waskow, I. E., 33
"We bond," 87–89
Weil, E., 138
Weiss, J., 22, 108, 126, 128, 170, 228